Speaking of Architecture

Interviews about practice, discourse,
and what comes next

by
Mark Foster Gage

EDITIONS
Novato, CA

Contents

Acknowledgments

by Mark Foster Gage

This book began as a seminar I taught at the Yale School of Architecture titled "Emerging Schools of Thought" during one of the remote semesters of the COVID-19 crisis. The intent of the course was to treat as an asset the seeming liability of having to teach via video, by embracing the recent global acceptance of virtual meetings. Capitalizing on a seeming abundance of COVID-19 quarantine free-time for scheduling meetings, I organized a weekly interview with architects to discuss, live with the students, the development of their careers, the state of their practices, and their thoughts on the future. The greatest acknowledgment needs to go to these students who braved not only yet another remote semester of learning but were willing to go along with such an experiment in lieu of what would normally be considered a seminar. The students, all part of the Yale Master of Architecture II graduate program, were: Vicky Achnani, Claudia Ansorena, Elise Barker Limon, Bobby Cheng, Stav Dror Shachaf, Samar Halloum, Bingyu He, Lillian Hou, Vignesh Krishnan, Ingrid Liu, Sydney Maubert, Serge Saab, Saba Salekfard, Steven Sculco, Yuyi Shen, Taiga Taba, Vivian Wu, Jiaxing Yan, Joon Yun, and Yuyi Zhou. Co-leading this endeavor was the teaching assistant who also became both the book designer and managing editor, Chris Pin, who had also worked in my office and was familiar with the ideas being discussed. At the time I was also supervising a PhD student who was part of the Yale / University College of London program, Marie Williams, who offered wonderful insight to the discussions and worked with the students individually to process at a more personal level some of the ideas that emerged during the interviews. This unique course could only have been possible through the continued support for creative ideas by the Yale School of Architecture leadership: Dean Deborah Berke, Associate Dean Phil Bernstein, Associate Dean Sunil Bald, and the key figures of the M. Arch II program of which these students were a part: Joel Sanders, Aniket Shahane, and Bimal Mendes, to name only a few. Of course, very special thanks to the contributors who were willing to be interviewed, published, and have their work put into the world in this format as part of this project. They are Michael Young (Young & Ayata); Elena Manferdini (Atelier Manferdini); Florencia Pita (Florencia Pita & Co.); Ferda Kolatan (su11 architecture+design); Amina Blacksher (Atelier Amina) and V. Mitch McEwen (Atelier Office); Tom Wiscombe (Tom Wiscombe Architecture); Kristy Balliet (BairBalliet); Ellie Abrons, Adam Fure, Meredith Miller, and Tom Moran (T+E+A+M); Jiminez Lai (Bureau Spectacular); and Karel Klein and David Ruy (Ruy Klein). I'd also like to thank Gordon Goff and Jake Anderson at ORO Editions for seeing the value of such a project and working so hard to see it documented in this book. A personal thanks to Jarron Magallanes, Gizmo, and Truman for their support and for putting up with a year of amplified Zoom calls from the adjacent room.

Foreword

by Greg Lynn

First, about Mark Foster Gage, the editor of this book. Any introduction of a book edited by Mark requires an in-depth history followed by a clear picture of the present. This is what is so important about his collection of figures and positions: historical depth and contemporary reflection. Personally, I discovered architecture at the end of a period where architecture was dominated by corporate Modernism; a time when Tom Wolf, Prince Charles, and Christopher Alexander were celebrated by 1980s cynical dandies for their pillorying of architects who had adopted the language of Le Corbusier and Mies van der Rohe. Because of this reactionary moment, I had the good fortune to be taught by what might best be referred to as historical post-Modernists who were educated by precedent and had conducted grand tours of Europe, all in conjunction with teaching design studios. Architectural history courses were abundant and required and I was taught to recognize hundreds, if not thousands, of buildings—and was quizzed to recognize them by either their plan organizations or through single photographs of their facades. It was a great time to be a sponge for historical information and, other than Robert A. M. Stern, who certainly knew one when he saw one, I never met a fellow sponge so moisturized with knowledge of architectural history than Mark Foster Gage.

As quickly as I experienced this moment of the relevance of architectural history rediscovered for present application, like an enormous souffle, this pedagogy collapsed both culturally and architecturally. Its main proponents abandoned ship and were relegated to the most conservative corners of the field. Post-Modernism retreated to the Hamptons and Disney theme parks; two places where you can still blend in while wearing a bow tie. Many post-Modernists survived by backing off excesses of history while sliding into tastefully refined historicism or high-end modernism realized in more luxurious materials. The real action moved into the future. Two decades of experiments with digital technology followed.

Sandwiched between historical post-Modernism of the early 1980s and the digital of the late 1990s you find an abyss, as most designers located themselves at either end of the spectrum but never in between. In my first year teaching at Yale, however, I met the single occupant of this seeming chasm, Mark Foster Gage—who I would go on to teach seven studios with over my seventeen years at the school. Of his generation, Mark is unique in his ability to compose from a contemporary manual of digital operations and transformations, while unlike his colleagues, he is also able to point these tools towards historical precedents that recall culturally received languages and practices, so they resonate with familiarity and discursive depth, all while retaining their slick gloss of the new. I hope this communicates the fact that this is disturbing to almost everyone in the discipline.

In this regard, Mark is in very good company with others who seek new fusions between history and a contemporary and technologically enabled form of design practice. The colleagues with whom he is in good company are contributors and interlocutors of this publication alongside new figures that must be recognized as part of the discourse of today. Perhaps ironically, there is historic precedent for this genre of "transitional" practitioners such as Josef Hoffman, Charles Rennie Mackintosh, Eliel Saarinen, Victor Horta, Bruno Taut, Antoni Gaudi, and many others who similarly jumped headlong into new materials and technologies while remaining planted in historic discourse and professional disciplinarity. Neither fish nor fowl, these designers were as influential as they were idiosyncratic. The one thing they all were, and that they share with Mark, was that their work was historically situated, and yet specific to a contemporary moment. A generation of designers without this knowledge of history and discourse has suffered from a situation where their work has been justified only through their application of the digital technologies of the present, as they assumed that digital tools are good for anything everywhere. Mark Foster Gage and many of the protagonists in this book have avoided this pitfall through a combined knowledge of how the past and present intersect, and perhaps equally as important, their ongoing discussions with each other … a behind-the-scenes glimpse which is the subject of this important book.

Often in the digital studios of the last three decades vocational training in the latest software is prioritized over cultural and social reception, leading to a disconnect between technological innovation and cultural relevance. What is most exceptional about Mark Foster Gage and this book is their undeclared search for a bridge that links the architectural discourses of the past, present, and future. This struggle to situate work with historical precedent must come from a desire to communicate with an audience in ways that resonate with the significance of historic canon, but instead use contemporary forms. The tensions between the editor and some contributors' commitment to disciplinary history and colleagues who do not feel this is a necessity is what makes this publication so interesting. This publication is extremely timely in its efforts to capture these tensions, and I can think of no better person to be able to capture the debates of this emerging generation than Mark Foster Gage.

Introduction

by Mark Foster Gage

"A veritable witness have you hitherto been, Ishmael; but have a care how you seize the privilege of Jonah alone; the privilege of discoursing upon the joists and beams; the rafters, ridge-pole, sleepers, and underpinnings, making up the framework of Leviathan…"

— Herman Melville, Moby Dick
(Chapter 102, "A Bower in the Arsacides")

This book explores the importance of discussion between architects as an overlooked but defining aspect of the discipline of architecture, and therefore the design of our world. No creative disciplines occur in a vacuum, but architecture's need for communication is particularly significant, relying as it does on numerous players and bodies of information including the more obvious professional expertise and construction knowledge—but also knowledge of history, technology, and a nearly two-millennia-long dialogue with theory, philosophy, and the world of ideas—also known as *discourse*. Philosophy and theory are often thought of as ancillary, even extraneous, to the discipline of architecture, especially today, and yet they are among the first subjects listed as requirements for practice in, quite literally, the first lines of the first chapter of the first book ever written about architecture, *De Architectura*, or the *Ten Books of Architecture*, by Roman architect Marcus Pollio Vitruvius in 30 BCE. As such this book accepts as an axiom that moral knowledge and engagement with philosophy, through discussion, are inseparable from the discipline of architecture.

The discussions featured in this book cover a wide range of emerging intellectual territories in architecture ranging from Speculative Realism, high vs. low resolution, neo-primitivism, artificial intelligence, philosophies of care, the post-digital, and new forms of social engagement, to name only a small sample. Architects whom I interviewed represent very different, even opposing, positions. They included Michael Young (Young & Ayata), Elena Manferdini (Atelier Manferdini); Florencia Pita (Florencia Pita & Co.); Ferda Kolatan (su11 architecture+design); Amina Blacksher (Atelier Amina) and V. Mitch McEwen (Atelier Office); Tom Wiscombe (Tom Wiscombe Architecture); Kristy Balliet (BairBalliet); Ellie Abrons, Adam Fure, Meredith Miller, and Tom Moran (T+E+A+M); Jiminez Lai (Bureau Spectacular); and Karel Klein and David Ruy (Ruy Klein).

So, here's the hard part—who gets to "speak" for architecture? There is of course no acceptable answer to this question, but it can also not be doubted that some voices and ideas have more impact in the world than others. Historically, new ideas and their introduction into architecture by the few have consistently and dramatically altered the output of each generation of the architectural many—in due course. That is to say that while the days of 'star-architecture' and hero-worship in the profession may today be briefly passe, architecture will likely always have figures at the forefront of some form of architectural "newness" that will, if history is any judge, continue to have an outsized impact on the built environments of the future—even if only eventually.

While many architects are uncomfortable with the concept of progressive thought leaders in the profession who haven't necessarily built much, architecture has always had such a vanguard of such emerging practitioners who push hard against the status quo, trying to redefine and improve what architecture is and can be. This is as true today as it was in ancient Rome when Vitruvius (who was actually a military ballistics engineer and had built almost nothing), called for revolutionary methods of employing Greco-Roman classicism to produce entirely new genres of urbanism that would eventually format entire continents. Le Corbusier began writing about his now-famous "Five Points" in the publication *L'Esprit Nouveau* in the early 1920s, at a time when he had only built a few houses—and all entirely in traditional styles. That is to say that innovative ideas tend to appear within architectural discourse long before they impact the built environment, or, in reverse, achievement in getting buildings built is rarely indicative of contributions to architectural discourse.

The conversations in this book likely tilt towards my own ambition to directly address the perceivable aspects of architecture as they are manifest in form, instead of humoring conceptual claims so frequently and casually made by architects that are entirely unrelated to actual design—or similar claims of architecture as policy making or other invisible formless endeavors that have recently found purchase in a small handful of architectural schools. Accordingly, this book is heavily illustrated by actual design work done by the actual architects being interviewed. I believe it is only through the combination of words and design work together that convincing architectural arguments are ever made. There will likely be pushback to this, as part of today's master-cliché is that the boundaries of the discipline have been expanded far beyond mere antiquated ideas of "building" to include, well, nearly everything. This may be true if we allow it to be … but if this is the case, who is then responsible for the built environment? If architects become the diagrammers of policy, curators of content, and creatives behind virtual experiences—who is designing the physical aspects of the real world that we all inhabit? While the figures I selected to interview offer extremely varied viewpoints, they all share an interest in architecture as thought and design made towards the production of form. This, therefore, is a book about how ideas actually shape architecture, not how non-architectural ideas shape more non-architectural ideas in order to be eternally celebrated as genius-powered expansions of the boundaries of architecture.

While this position draws a clear boundary around the discipline and discourse of architecture, it does not seek to in any way diminish the responsibility of architects to act towards ethical and moral ends. All architects have the responsibility, through any discursive position, to address humanitarian concerns in all their many valences including issues of health, sustainability, equality, community engagement, and the pursuit of the just. None of these ambitions conflict with discussions about form, shape, the design of physical things—or, dare I say, their aesthetics. One criticism often levied against architects with an interest in the design of form is that in doing so they are not solving the larger social and political problems of the world. I don't see that these ambitions are mutually exclusive. In fact, I worry that architects who claim to *not* be interested in mere form and are in favor of *only* socially performative ambitions are, by definition, defaulting to the status quo of standard practices for the deployment of forms and materials in the world. That is to say that architects who claim not to be interested in form are merely showcasing their support for the status quo of form production—and thus shouting their willingness to cede control of the design of form and materials to the established economically driven system of pure capitalist architectural production. Put another way, if an architect is *not* addressing the physical manifestations of form in their design work they are not remaining neutral, but rather are accepting that the architectural forms naturally produced by the economics of capitalism are sufficient for human needs. If architects do not design the *form* of our built environment, economic spreadsheets with a sole concern for profit will. Nearly any late-20th-century city can attest to the abject failure of such a disciplinary retreat.

Knowledge about the current landscape of discourse-oriented practices featured in this book is intended to be of particular use to students and emerging practitioners of architecture, as they hold the future of architectural discourse in their hands. Its continued existence is not a given, but rather requires the continued contributions of every subsequent generation. These future contributions, however, must be informed, and their authors can only be empowered through having knowledge of the landscape of architectural innovation and discussion into which they are entering. This book will hopefully allow such students and practitioners to position their work as such within a context of current and emerging architectural movements, ideas, technologies, and, at times, conflicts and arguments, as they continue the ongoing two-millennia-long conversation that arises from the seemingly small act of thinking, writing, and ultimately speaking of architecture.

First Chapter

Artificial Intelligence in Architecture

Discussion with
Karel Klein and **David Ruy**
of Ruy Klein

artificial intelligence, reification and power, digital debris, facticity through technology, re-enchantment, mythology

David Ruy: You don't need me to tell you that something has changed. Though architecture has been talking about the crisis of the discipline since the 1960s, this time it feels real. Within the global pandemic that has so indelibly marked history now, technology has been playing a subtle but profound role in the emergency we face. We've come to a point of uncertainty about what is real and what is not. Facts co-mingle with fiction every day in both beautiful and terrifying ways. As the artist Hito, Steyerl says appropriately, "we're now living within a debris field of images." We live under the ever-present cloud of data and have difficulty resolving their reality with the facts, which we still nonetheless see on the ground. It's difficult to deny any longer that facts are constructed by institutions. With that realization and our heightened awareness now of colonialist legacies, it is so tempting to discard the problems of facticity altogether. But we also can't deny just how dangerous that really is. How we build new concepts around the problem of fact might very well be the most important intellectual problem of the century. In the world of architecture, I'm thinking of how normal it is today to use a Google image search to hunt for precedent images. I'm thinking of how institutions we once relied on to construct their histories have lost their influence of authority. I'm thinking about how we know the world more through our devices, like the phone in your pocket, right now than through books, museums, universities, or even firsthand experience. I'm thinking about how social media has become a primary instrument of cultural dissemination. It used to take a long time to get to know or develop a form and a style. Today, we might type in some words like "Le Corbusier + Five Points" and get back 1.7 million results in 0.62 seconds. Most of the images retrieved when we search in this way are copies of copies of copies. What does originality even mean anymore in this context? Who is retrieving these images for us? How should we use them? What are we to do with the surplus? Viktor Shklovsky once argued that great works of art do their work by familiarizing normal reality and slowing down habits of perception and the beholder. Similarly, but with regard to the difficulty of authoring great works, Harold Bloom would later on assert in *The Anxiety of Influence* that masterpieces are nothing more than creative misinterpretations or misprisions of previous masterpieces. Maybe the new question for us is how such theories of estrangement are to be understood when it is not the human author doing the reading, writing, seeing, or imaging, but a machine author. Even more convoluted is the very same question relative to a hybrid human machine author. Though this may sound strange to you, I am interested in asking how a cyborg might design architecture. I would like to think more about the possibilities of

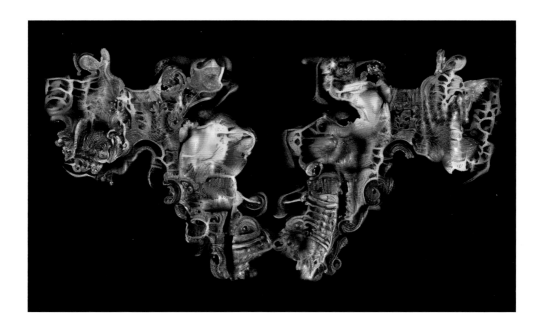

a cyborg misprision. This question should not be taken as some silly scenario—becoming a robot designer as kitsch science fiction might like to imagine—because as Donna Haraway points out in *A Cyborg Manifesto*, "we are already cyber."

Mark Foster Gage: You know, there are doctors who can put their hands on a patient's chest to feel their heart in order to find out whether they are alive or not. Then, there are those doctors who can put one finger in some specific place on the neck and tell you if you have a heart murmur or something really difficult to detect. It requires a combination of expertise and a heightened level of sensitivity to be the latter kind of doctor. The two of you have always been that latter kind of doctor when it comes to architectural discourse. You both have always had a very savvy ability to navigate not only the contemporary topics but also what the contemporary topics are going to be. As mentioned, you're dealing with a lot of things—everything from Artificial Intelligence to Formalism to Politics—and that's really a wide spectrum to tie together. How did you end up with these interests, as architects today, and what were the ideas that impacted you or pushed you in these directions at any point in your educations or careers? As a follow up I'd also like to know how you think your interest in discourse changed with the advent of these new technologies like Artificial Intelligence. Which

comes first, the chicken or the egg? Does the technology produce the discourse or does the discourse absorb the technology? In short, how did you become you, discursively? And dare I ask…Do you consider yourself, regarding these technologies, to be a formalist?

David Ruy: In architecture, we use the term "formalism" without much consciousness of its complex history during the 20th century. In order to think about what formalism might mean in the 21st century, it might be good to think about its origins during the early days of the Soviet Union. What's remembered today as Russian formalism was a new way of reading a text. Instead of focusing on social contacts and traditions of interpretation, the formalists proposed looking carefully at the text itself. No need to understand the author's intentions or identity, everything you needed was right there in the text. Though the formalists and their procedures were initially vital to the ambitions of forging a new society from nothing, this tension intensified almost immediately with the material realism of the Marxists. Less than two decades into the new history of the Soviet Union Stalin would eradicate formalism from the communist state, declaring formalism subversive and counter revolutionary. No more black squares; in its place portraits of Stalin receiving flowers from children. During the Congress of 1934 four guidelines were laid out for

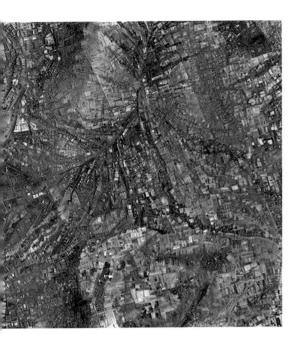

Soviet Union. This flip-flopping of formalism and realism remains a fascinating curiosity in the history of the Cold War. The strange history of formalism versus realism and its uses by both the left and the right can even be seen today in the ongoing debate regarding textualism versus pragmatism in jurisprudence at the United States Supreme Court. What should be noticed is that formalists, whether it is Viktor Shklovsky or Neil Gorsuch, have used these procedures to make a break with the immediate past. Realism, on the other hand, has been the primary strategy of turning art into a political instrument of the ruling ideology—a tool of maintaining the status quo of power. In our current moment, as we want to make a break with the past, and my God who doesn't, isn't it surprising to think that formalism might be the more useful instrument? I'm not suggesting making black squares again, though it's not that Malevich was wrong in this procedure originally. The problem today is when we see a black square we see Malevich. If we were to reinvest in a formalism, I think it has to be a weird formalism. For formalism to do its work it needs to be unrecognizable as a formalism.

Karel Klein: We've evolved from a very early interest in the relationship of architecture to nature, to more recent ideas regarding artificial nature. David actually just started a new program at SCI-Arc titled *Synthetic Landscapes* that parallels

this new socialist-realist art. The new art would have to be 1) Proletarian; art relevant to the workers and understandable to them, 2) Typical; scenes of everyday life of the people. 3) Realistic, in the representational sense, and 4) Partisan; supportive of the aims of the state and the party. Despite ironic parallels between this new state art with the art of the WPA in the United States, the art of formalism and this idea of abstraction would soon find the most unlikely patron in the United States CIA, culminating in the New American Painting exhibition in 1958, promoting an abstract expressionism and its implicit message— the superiority of free American culture in contrast to the totalitarian banality of the

Discussion with
Karel Klein and **David Ruy of Ruy Klein**

our own exploration of these ideas. All these interests evolve relative to technology. I can't speak for David, but my current interest is in how language and the qualities of imagery that come from AI technologies allow for a different kind of architectural imagination, for an enchantment of the world. There is some marginal discourse out there about a re-enchantment of the world through artifacts like architecture and other creative mediums, and this has been a thread that has been intrinsic to my own interests over the years, ever since I first read Bataille. That might account for a difference in how David and I are each leaning into artificial intelligence technologies. I've also become very interested in the thinker Roger Caillois, who coined the phrase "diagonal science." He was very interested in that space between fact and the imaginable, and cutting across multiple disciplines of science would enable him to propose unusual ideas. I think the best example of that is his text "Mimicry and Legendary Psychasthenia" where he speaks about insect mimicry and concludes by discussing a psychotic relationship to space where you lose your sense of self through losing your sense of edges, which becomes a spatial and architectural idea. Insect mimicry connected to ideas about psychotic space is something that could only come from cutting across multiple disciplines.

Mark Foster Gage: David, how are your interests different?

David Ruy: Karel and I met at Columbia while we were both in graduate school and the thing we shared as an instinct back then was an interest in the sublime. We still share that as a motivation and desire to some extent. However, the more we tried to unravel what that intuition was about relative to the sublime, the more our positions became divergent. The void we started diving into was very wide, and two domains became quite clear regarding this aesthetic experience; one was through technology and the other was through nature. Nature is the older domain of the

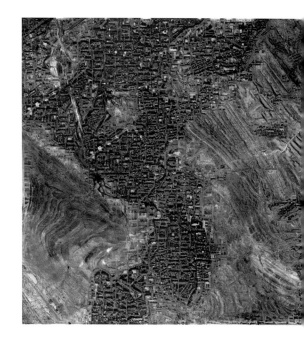

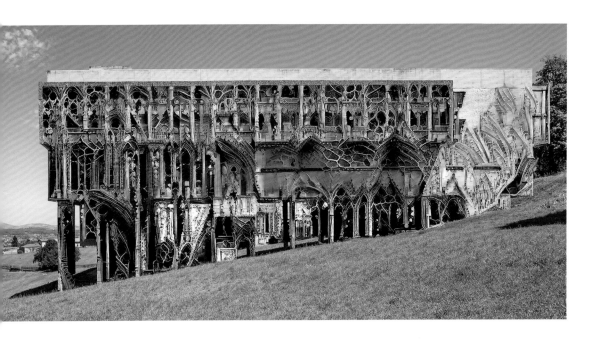

sublime, such as that found in the unknowable and infinite space. You see this in paintings such as Caspar David Friedrich's *Wanderer above the Sea of Fog*. Later on, I would discover people like Leo Marx and David Nye, who both write really beautifully about how this idea of a natural sublime changed dramatically in the 20th century, particularly in the United States. He describes how this experience of the sublime evolves to have more to do with technological events, as opposed only to nature. When you go to the beach, you might look at the ocean and feel traces of the sublime, but hardly—we are all pretty disenchanted in that way. Now, if you saw an actual nuclear explosion, you would most definitely feel the sublime. Of course,

that's a product of technology. It's the same feeling you get when you go to the Hoover Dam, that's what makes it so impressive. Nature rarely captures the sublime anymore, because you got the park rangers kiosk over there and you've got the tractor over there and you got the oil pump over there. All these traces of human existence have the effect of alienating a sense of the sublime or enchantment in nature.

Mark Foster Gage: That idea of enchantment is something that the Enlightenment unknowingly ended. And then in our own field, architecture, modernism did even more to remove enchantment from the equation of perception because it so focused on seeing the truth of a thing, on

Discussion with
Karel Klein and **David Ruy of Ruy Klein**

transparency, on clear structure, etc. All these efforts to reveal things found in modernism are at odds—if not simply the complete opposite—with an architecture acting to encourage mystery or enchantment through design. You also mentioned this idea of the liminal space between fact and fiction. I'm struck at how supremely relevant those ideas are now in our politics. Just yesterday Liz Cheney was ousted from her leadership position in the Republican house because she didn't believe in the fiction that the election between Donald Trump and Joe Biden was stolen by the latter. In fact, 70% of Republicans still believe that the election was stolen, and fealty to that fiction is what's driving our political situation right now. What seemed to many to be frivolous eight years ago, when we were talking about how fiction and facts are intertwining in architecture, through things like counterfactual and parafictional design practices, have now become the defining characteristic of our politics. Fiction has become the basis of our political system at the moment. It's interesting that you're not just addressing such ideas through words, but through design, which I think is a very difficult thing to do. Somewhat related to this, as I know many of these ideas are things you've refined through discussion with other people, can you speak at all about how the ideas of mentors or peers shaped your trajectory and development as architects? Did you have people that really supercharged your interests, supercharged your careers, or opened certain opportunities for you?

Karel Klein: The idea of mentors lives in a memory that is fallible, so for me, it's hard to remember impactful relationships with mentors. I would say that the relationships with peers have been far more significant. It helps to have friends who are insanely talented and brilliant and to surround yourself with people who are thinking, not just in ways that you are yourself, but also challenging your thoughts. People like Mark are important in this sense, and there's been many more over time. I think it's important to cultivate a group of colleagues and cultivate those peer networks.

It's important to make the discourse a part of your social life.

Mark Foster Gage: I remember having a conversation about the sublime around 2008 with David and we didn't really know each other yet. Around the time, I had this really focused interest in aesthetics, and nobody else was talking about aesthetics. Of course, the sublime is very much within the discourse of aesthetics, so I felt a kind of kindred interest that was nourished in the way that Karel was describing. Architectural discourse was becoming something that was no longer separate from my social life. I have to say over the years I've argued, learned, debated, and constructed more architectural discourse at late-night dinners than I ever

Discussion with
Karel Klein and **David Ruy of Ruy Klein**

have at symposia or more official academic events. David, do you have thoughts on this?

David Ruy: The only people I would really point to as mentors would probably be more in my undergraduate education at St. John's College in Annapolis where Graham Harman and I were classmates. He and I actually shared the same mentors while we were there, interestingly. In our cases, it had more to do with finding a way to live a life of the mind, how to live a life where you're thinking all the time and developing and being committed to thought. It wasn't a Christian school but there was an Irish Christian brother who just happened to teach there, and he was an expert on hermeneutics. I remember he was missing an index finger, which I later found out was from a wine press accident when he was a child. Anyway, he had this habit of pointing with this invisible finger. He was the one that really sparked this idea that I could be a philosopher, the idea that this was actually a pursuit in the world that's arguably more important than simply making a livable wage. He made me realize that it might be something I could take more seriously.

Mark Foster Gage: Just this week I've been reading Petrarch's "Secretum," from the mid-14th century and came across this line where he says, "What's the good of singing sweetly to others if you can't listen to yourself." I think this idea of the life of the mind as an architect involves quite a bit of introspection, which people don't normally associate with architecture. It's interesting to hear how it's been such an important part of not only your practice but your lives.

David Ruy: As Karel mentioned, I also believe that peers have been absolutely critical to our development as architects and thinkers. Architectural discourse used to be very hierarchical and I think that's something that very much changed, something that has been brought about by peer relations rather than mentor relations. Our generation of architects were part of this transition. We saw that power structure unraveling as we were developing our early careers. That may have had the unintended effect of leaving students and young architects in a funny position where now it's expected that you make it on your own. There are days, no matter how old you are, when you wish you had someone to advise you and to take you through things, but we're in a different culture now where that is less valued. This new world of architectural discourse is infinitely more difficult to navigate but also, of course, there are more opportunities.

Mark Foster Gage: I had a discussion as part of this series with Jimenez Lai and Kristy Balliet, who talked about that unraveling of power structures in architecture through their *Possible Mediums* conference, which occurred at Ohio State

related to the various conference topics at the same time. That really empowers students to be able to make original contributions to the discourse. Such an important part of discourse today is this equalizing of the profession and abandoning of historic power structures within it. This addresses those who are in positions of architectural privilege, but it also includes those who get to publish, and those who determine things like "canon."

Steven Sculco: Could you speak about your experiences as educators, and how you bounce ideas off of students and learn with them in a sense?

David Ruy: I think it was inevitable that Karel and I would end up teaching at SCI-Arc. SCI-Arc was a school founded by hippies in 1973 because they hated the way that universities operated. The hippies actually turned out to be some pretty important architects, like Thom Mayne. From the school's inception it was intended to be the anti-university, although it later became successful and it has since become more university-esque. What is and has always been unique about SCI-Arc is that it acts as an incubator of ideas about the future of architecture. In order to really answer this question, I think it would be good to unpack a bit about the history of the university as an idea. The idea of a university is not something that's founded in Athens, as people sometimes like to think. The university was really founded in the 16th

in 2013. It was a launching-pad for many of their careers. This conference was important because the students were the ones making the contributions just as much as any of the faculty. It had a heavy workshop component associated with the symposium aspect, so students were making things

century at the University of Bologna in Italy. Shortly thereafter emerged universities in Paris and at Oxford in the UK. The creation of the university was kind of an accident, connected to the history of the Jewish diaspora. There was a significant Jewish community and mercantile class in Bologna and they basically banded together to help each other, through education. They would hire learned people to teach them law and various other things, but then the government saw what was going on and realized it was gaining momentum, so they quickly took command of its development. It's an interesting idea in human history that there would be a specific space in society for the making, and permanent stewardship, of knowledge. There's a unique firewall between commercial and political interests, and what's done at the university by design. It was designed in Western society to be that way and then it spread all over the world as a model. It's been interesting for a school like SCI-Arc to be that anti-anti society, in a sense. If the university was the original anti-marketplace, what does it mean to be the anti-university?

Mark Foster Gage: Good question. The context in which we all operate is something that we do not really discuss too much. It's like fish in water; they don't notice the water because they've been in

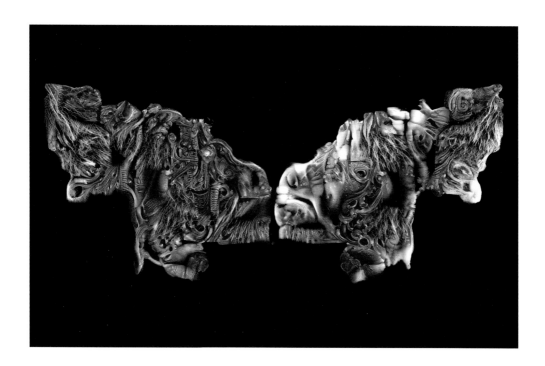

were supposed to have this firewall, have become dependent for their resources on the thing they were supposed to be protected from; the influence of the marketplace. How would you define the differences in how you two teach?

David Ruy: I think I'm more in the minority of SCI-Arc, meaning I don't want my students to do what I do. I'm very happy to share my knowledge with my students and show them what I know how to do, but it doesn't excite me to have them copy my work. I don't quite understand why it would be of value for them to mimic what I do. I generally encourage individuality and I try to get them to construct an identity for themselves. I think that is the most important way to navigate our current cultural economy; if you're like somebody else you're not valuable. Copies are not as valuable as originals.

Karel Klein: I don't teach what I know, rather I am trying to figure out what I want to discover and the studio space becomes a laboratory toward that end. Sometimes I speak to my students about engaging the imagination to a greater degree, that they are part of an experimental laboratory of ideas, and that they are testing things that might not have been explored anywhere before. This, however, often means that I'm teaching things that I've never done before either. Sometimes very new tools are a part of this exploration. When I first started working with these Artificial

it their whole lives. I've taught at Yale since 2001, and here the situation is a bit of a loaded condition because that historic firewall is more of a porous shredded membrane. You can't be sitting on a $30 billion endowment and still consider yourself anti-marketplace. I think this may be a reason that Yale has a bit more of a conservative stance in its architecture school than places like SCI-Arc. If the goal is to design architecture that changes the world, that's great for SCI-Arc and less great for Yale, because who knows if that $30 billion will still mean the same thing in whatever new world is developed. It's a particularly American trend, that Universities that

Discussion with
Karel Klein and **David Ruy of Ruy Klein**

Intelligence technologies, they were brand new, so it was really just a process of trying to figure them out. I'm not sharing existing knowledge in the way that David does as a teacher. He's a storyteller in a way, in terms of those things that he knows about. A good example is his earlier description of the history of universities. The things that I find compelling can be very difficult to describe to students, so they might think, "I don't know what the hell she's talking about, but she's excited about something." In that way, I'm more of a mad scientist.

Mark Foster Gage: I have a question about your Artificial Intelligence work. You discover this technology and you already have this personal interest in what you've called the re-enchantment of the world. You might describe this as reintroducing curiosity or wonder in things, and you then merge the two in this idea of artificial imagination. In using AI to think of things that the human mind cannot think of, does that naturally makes them more enchanting? Or is there some other way that AI plays specifically into your overall theoretical or formal agenda?

Karel Klein: AI can produce all sorts of images that are simultaneously impossible to decipher, illegible, painterly, but also very precise, very photo real, very articulate, and very intricate. In the beginning of this research I was particularly compelled by the images that had that Freudian uncanny quality. The images seemed familiar, yet they were clearly and disturbingly showing you something that you hadn't seen before. You definitely have that sensation of, "Holy shit is this thing that I'm looking at actually in the world?" These images have such precision that you can study them as real. You could hold a magnifying glass up to this image and see exactly how it's articulated, almost as if you were looking at a physical tectonic architectural detail. That was a re-enchantment in a way, a fantastic impossible possibility. It created the desire to understand a quasi-mythical relationship through artifacts that aren't necessarily places, but potential architectures.

Mark Foster Gage: That's a criticism that's often levied against this type of work, that it's not yet real architecture, that if something can't be immediately constructed using the corporate products of today then it doesn't count as "architecture." What's so bizarre about this belief is that all of the buildings of today, particularly in New York City's growing collection of banal glass box skyscrapers, are all considered architecture with no questions asked. Anything slightly more speculative is not. However, it was almost exactly a century ago, in 1921, when Mies Van Der Rohe sketched out his speculative Friedrichstrasse Skyscraper Project, which was, at the time, an "unbuildable" glass tower. Let's take a glass box in Manhattan that just went up with the stupid little twist

Discussion with
Karel Klein and **David Ruy of Ruy Klein**

in it, and compare it to Mies's speculative Friedrichstrasse project. The former was built and the latter never was. Which one influenced a century of building designs? Which one is more real? Which had more of an impact, as architecture, on the development of global cities, and on the appearance of our very urban realities? Undoubtedly, the never-built speculative project rather than the one that was built.

Karel Klein: Speculation today also has the opportunity to be more than just object making, it can be about a re-mythologizing and re-ritualizing of things in the world. It is not just about an object, but also a shift in how we think about culture, how we think about history, and how we might think about other kinds of disciplines of knowledge differently, including architecture.

David Ruy: You know Mark, I don't think I've told you this, but you are what triggered the whole deep dive into Artificial Intelligence. One day several years ago you texted me and Tom Wiscombe an image that was an AI-generated photograph of you as an old man. We all looked at it like, "Why the hell is Mark an 80-year-old?" Of course, we eventually discovered it was just a new iPhone app that allowed you to age differently or change gender. But there was something strange about the photorealism of it. I knew there was something really weird going on, and wanted to know more about how that image of 80-year-old you was being generated. I did a deep

dive into the processes within the app and discovered that they were using a convolutional neural network, using a database of thousands of faces. The more I investigated the more I realized, "Holy crap this is going to be utterly game-changing in how we produce images.

Mark Foster Gage: So you're saying I'm the Godfather of artificial intelligence in architecture? I had no idea...It was when apps were pretty new and I was just downloading tons to see what they could do. It

was a whole world of expertise that just got placed into our hands, literally. The ones most downloaded were the ones that were for fun—like the face app. I probably played with that one for hours. Just be glad I didn't send you some of the others. The only thing I ended up learning is that it would just be best for me to not age. The real takeaway here is that I stumbled on this face app, I thought it was hilarious, I sent it to you and some other friends, and it prompted something. I often get

Discussion with
Karel Klein and **David Ruy of Ruy Klein**

criticism for using tools that don't seem particularly useful to architecture, but AI is undoubtedly revolutionizing specific boundaries of our reality in ways we can't even imagine. We have a choice as architects to either start to engage with AI right now, or to stick our heads in the sand. The problem with starting to engage with new technology is that you don't know where it's going to lead, which is why Karel, you were speaking about your studios being a laboratory. There's no set discourse of information that you can give to students about how AI enters into architecture, so you have to take a leap of faith to teach it. It's opening yourself up to criticism, but that's the nature of experimentation.

David Ruy: I would stake my reputation on the line and say that AI is going to be the most important technology to think about for the next 100 years. It's absolutely clear to me, and it has everything to do with facts commingling with fiction. We started out talking about how this is happening through a technological substrate, considering social media and what our tools of communication have done to political discourse. Amazon is figuring out what everybody wants to buy and they have started a practice of shipping objects toward you using a predictive AI-based algorithm constructed from your past shopping patterns even before you've ordered it.

Mark Foster Gage: That is such a spatial idea as well and architects should absolutely

be addressing it. All of that process takes warehouses, which impacts urban development. It all has such high-stakes spatial consequences. This is what a lot of Keller Easterling's writing is about, how these systems of space production are happening almost unchecked and without architectural intelligence. She's asking us to think about design of not only these buildings, like warehouses, but to start thinking about the design of the medium—of something like the very notion of delivery itself. All of these things come through constructed space at one point or another. It's funny, I co-taught an advanced studio with Graham Harman at Yale last year, and to this day I still get ads from all sorts of companies with merchandise that has Graham and Mark embroidered with a heart around it. These AI programs are seeing that Graham Harman and I are mentioned in the same places all over the internet so they assume we're a couple. A couple of times a month I get these ads for Graham and Mark embroidered bathroom towels, or Graham and Mark printed pillows. It's exciting but also a little bit terrifying.

Karel Klein: Isn't it awesome that it makes those mistakes? It is kind of joyful in a way.

Mark Foster Gage: Until SKYNET launches a nuclear missile at us…

David Ruy: I'm a bit more of a pessimist. I believe that 99% of the utilization of AI

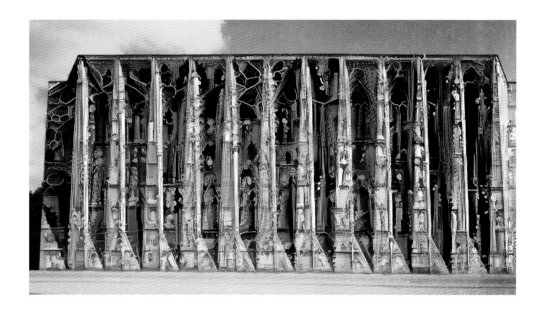

technology is going to be for the automation of human labor. We should not kid ourselves about that. It is not going to be creative. It will be used for the purposes of accumulating capital, and how that capital should be redistributed is something we need to be thinking about. For Karel and I, we're using it in a very different kind of way. We're making a pretty esoteric connection to theories of familiarization and essentially bringing in a degree of criticality into this technology, but that's not going to be its primary destiny. This is not the main way this technology will be used in architecture. To Mark's point, these targeted ads are moments that are meant to train people to think, "Oh AI is for Amazon, it's not for aesthetics," and that's precisely the point. It's the narrative that's being constructed by capital. Why would you want to agree with that? There has to be some form of resistance to that.

Karel Klein: This might sound like a non sequitur, but I am also curious about architecture as an object that perhaps, as explained by Walter Benjamin, is more of the kind of collector's object than the utilitarian capitalist object. If there is a kind of duality between objects—objects that are for utility versus objects that are for collecting—architecture may be that place where both kinds of aspects are shared. What's beautiful about the way Walter Benjamin talks about objects for collecting is that they end up being vessels for memory, vessels for these things that I talked about, for mythmaking and ritual.

Discussion with
Karel Klein and **David Ruy of Ruy Klein**

These technologies provide an entry point into the ways that architecture as objects can have that aspect of being, can be visualized, can be produced. This opposes the idea of architecture as only being a capitalist object. It becomes necessary for architecture to address these spatial consequences of AI as part of this larger capitalist machine.

Mark Foster Gage: This is similar to Oscar Wilde's idea about art. He's famous for saying that "all art is quite useless," not because he thought art was useless or without value, but because he wanted to give it zero value so it wouldn't become a part of the capitalist marketplace. He was trying to save art from the vulgarities of the newly developing consumerist society and thought that the only way art could survive separate from it was for it to have no value.

Karel Klein: That's beautiful.

Mark Foster Gage: Everyone assumes that quote, "all art is quite useless," is just Oscar Wilde saying that art is frivolous and that is completely backwards. He just wanted to just show that it had zero economic value so it couldn't be co-opted by capitalism, making it an object resistant to the marketplace. In our neo-liberal capitalist society there's a lot of architects thinking about how architecture in some ways can be resistant to the colonial, corporate, neo-liberal marketplace in which everything currently exists.

David Ruy: There's something very basic about our interest in these things. We are befuddled and perplexed by the vast banality of lived experience today and the alienation we all feel. This is why we've been using this term "enchantment." One of the downsides of critical theory is that it demystifies the world, and a good amount of that was necessary because the primary thing to demystify was power. There was this belief in critical theory that one shouldn't believe the stories that "power" tells you about why certain things are the way that they are. Critical theory wanted to become an instrument for deconstructing and demystifying that power in the early to mid-20th century. One of the problems with this is that when there is non-stop demystification of everything, in every hour of every day, what does that result in? It results in an alienated existence that makes you think, "I'm not connected to anything in the world." The world becomes this debris field of meaninglessness. How we read and share the world is an important political problem right now. For instance, our daughter has an app on her iPad where you can point at the sky and see the constellations. She will point the iPad to the sky and there will be animals and warriors and all these figures. I only see planets orbiting the sun, distant stars millions of light years away, and the chemical composition of fusion reaction. This has utterly demystified the experience of life, and I think it sets up a great problem; how do we re-enchant the world?

Mark Foster Gage: Santiago Calatrava's transit station in New York City is an example of that demystification happening in architecture. It's made to look like a child's hand releasing a dove, and once that is explained to you, it's a form of architectural demystification. When you tell someone what the building is "about" they get it instantly, they feel like they don't have to know anything else about it and they don't have any curiosity that would take them to a deeper level. One of the values of enchantment is that it invites curiosity, it encourages you to go deeper into the thing that you're being presented with. It can raise your sensitivity to reality.

David Ruy: This is a very important problem for the architect because we've always had a problematic relationship to power. Architecture is generally what people think of when they are thinking about what reality is. I can't recall the last time I've been in a frontier where civilization hasn't touched something yet. You'll see a research station that might still have wi-fi even on the North Pole. It's really the built environment that constructs reality and I would like to see that change. I would like to see a lived experience that isn't banal.

Mark Foster Gage: Once these AI technologies enter an architecture in a way that impacts the physical construction of the world, what is your hope? Or do you think it always stays non-physical in architecture?

David Ruy: It's already too late in regard to architecture, because that's precisely what we're doing here today right now. What is new is determined by institutional discourse, the very fact that we're conducting institutional discourse right now and speaking about AI, has made it real.

Mark Foster Gage: Karel, if you now could talk to yourself as a graduating student or emerging architect interested in engaging with the discourse of today, in an architectural life of the mind, what kind of advice would you give?

Karel Klein: It's only been relatively recently that I've indulged my long-held interests in a way that is beyond pleasurable and satisfying. I don't know if my advice is to trust your instincts and indulge in interests early on, or instead to merely not dismiss the intuitions that you may have early on, because in my case it might have turned out better to have let them simmer or ferment for this long before they entered the world. Timing aside, I would absolutely tell them to trust their intuition and to feed their imagination. If you can trust your intuition, your ideas, and your thoughts as you engage in architecture and its discourse, and you surround yourself with brilliant people, then you can't lose.

Second Chapter

New Forms of
Social Engagement

Discussion with
V. Mitch McEwen and **Amina Blacksher**
of Atelier Office and Atelier Amina

designing the client, pre-design in practice,
practice is discourse, against pulling punches,
the assumptions of technology,
proprioceptive architecture

At the time of this interview, Amina Blacksher and Mitch McEwen
collaborated under the name Atelier Office. Amina Blacksher now works
under the moniker Atelier Amina.

Mark Foster Gage: In full disclosure, Amina was my student at Yale around 2010 so I have been following her trajectory through the profession. And Mitch, I became aware of your work most directly from your project for the 2016 Venice Biennale and more recently your project that exhibited at the Museum of Modern Art's recent Reconstructions: Blackness and Architecture in America exhibition. You two came together to form a practice recently, Atelier Office. Within this dialogue series that I'm doing I thought that, although you're a bit younger than most of the people I've been talking with, your story and body of work needed to be explored further. You two are bringing something to the table that is very different than what one would find in architectural discourse over the past decade or two. That is to say, a fresh perspective on the idea of practice as the site of innovation. I'd like to learn how you came about these interests of practice, the body, robotics being used for things other than fabrication, etc. You both have different backgrounds and haven't had a practice together for too long, so I'd like to get your thoughts individually and together about a few things.

Amina Blacksher: To give a brief overview, it's been about a year and a half since Mitch and I came together with the idea of the merger. We were in person when we made the toast, "Stronger together," and, "Yes, let's do it." Then, when we started to unpack and sketch a business plan, we were in different places. Over the past year, leading up to the launch of our work, I was in Brazil and then came to Florida where I've been since last March because of the pandemic. Collaborating over such long distances means that we've had to be really clear about who we are. We needed to get everything on paper, rather than just operating on assumptions. Being in the same room there's a level of familiarity that has to do with non-verbal communication. In the absence of that we've had to put it all in writing, as a dream spreadsheet, work for actual projects, and our business plan.

Mark Foster Gage: I saw the piece that Mitch did for the aforementioned blackness show at the MoMA and it's interesting to me that your combined practice has a wing of theoretical speculation as well as a kind of visionary counterfactual thinking. Your practice runs from one extreme to the other— from a modest project for a non-profit where it's all about practice and getting paid as an architectural firm, to a kind of theoretical, cultural, museum endeavor

about ideas of race and where we are now as a culture. I would be interested in how those two seemingly disparate poles come together in the future of your practice. How do you envision the relationship between, the scrappy, real world, low budget work versus the visionary ideas?

V. Mitch McEwen: I would flip that around because at some level clients and institutions are much more of an unknown animal, much more a conceptual beast than something like an installation or museum project. This is what any architect does right? It reminds me of a diagram that Ray Eames did, hatching over what the client is interested in, hatching over what the architect is interested in, and hatching over what

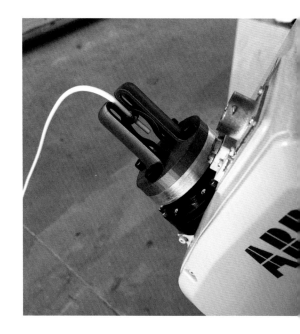

society needs. It speaks to how those ideas overlap and intersect. A museum project works at the level of ideation and content in the way that it challenges assumptions and norms. Whereas a client-based project like the one we're doing for the Miami Design District is just luxury presents luxury. We had to push on that latter one to get something else out of it. We're always pushing with our projects; I don't think it's something that just kind of arrives.

Mark Foster Gage: The majority of the other people we've interviewed had very strong, let's say, formal ambitions. The sense I get from your projects is that you're more interested in prying open how the architect interfaces with the client and finding opportunities in that relationship for practice. Your discursive interests are really similar to your professional interests, there's a lot of overlap. That is to say that the idea of practice, rather than form, affect, or performance, is the site of your research inquiry. Could you talk about that interest, or how that interest came about?

Amina Blacksher: It's important to have dreams that scare us, dreams where we don't know how it would be possible to achieve them. We've talked a lot about the way that we first came together; I wanted to produce a piece for the Black Imagination Matters conference that Mitch organized at Princeton University, and when I had my idea I said, "I don't know, this seems like

Discussion with
Mitch McEwen and **Amina Blacksher**

a crazy idea," and Mitch just said, "Do it." I had a lot of doubts, but as our office has fused this reluctance has changed. Now we are committing to everything, everything we do is architecture, everything is possible. Part of the process is expecting that there'll be hurdles. We know our existence is improbable and our success is improbable in a lot of the arenas that we want to operate in. Our practice and what we do is met with surprise or disbelief. That's important; that the impossible is just the starting point for us.

Mark Foster Gage: That's a great introduction to your collective idea about practice. What, as individuals, put you on course to work in the way that you are starting to work?

Amina Blacksher: To a certain degree, I'm still becoming. We are only at chapter two, maybe even at the end of chapter one. I can now see the differences between all the strategies that I've used to find resolve in myself, but they aren't so easily conveyed. I also have learned to gauge when it really matters, and for what audience, that I make myself into a performance.

V. Mitch McEwen: I've always been impressed with folks who build. I enjoy architectural discourse, but I feel like it's a useful hobby. Hobbies are important, and we can talk about that later, but it's not the only place that we can operate theoretically. Our backgrounds professionally factor into our practice as well. I worked for Bernard Tschumi before starting my own independent work and Amina worked for Bjarke Ingels. I never had the opportunity to work for a Bjarke Ingels-type of character, so I really appreciate that we bring different kinds of experiences into the studio. Bernard Tschumi was this very discursive figure who builds; and that is totally different from BIG, who builds for real estate developers. It's a convergence of two different sides.

Mark Foster Gage: That's an interesting collision of viewpoints, Bernard Tschumi versus Bjarke Ingels. I'm entirely aligned with the former, as I believe discourse, not fame, is what makes architecture culturally valuable. Beyond the professional experiences with these offices, how much of a boost do you get from other types of mentors and peers? Have there been any ideas you came across that really changed the direction of your thinking? I'm fascinated by the collisions between people and ideas, the flashbulb moments that send us off in different directions within practice.

Amina Blacksher: I really appreciate the apprentice/master model. Working for a long period of time under someone that you really admire. This goes back to the master builder and some similar ideas you find in West Africa. That experience had a major impact on me in terms of working on large buildings, getting comfortable with working on projects that would change a

skyline, understanding that impact and the public buy-in, as well as the buy-in from all the local architects and committees. I learned about all these negotiations you need to manage for a project at that scale. That experience was a big shift in the scale of projects I had previously worked on when I worked at Ennead and a smaller boutique firm, Gordon Kipping Architects, when I first came out of graduate school. During graduate school at Yale, there were also three people who were significant influences on me; you, Jennifer Liang, and Ariane Lourie-Harrison.

Mark Foster Gage: I hope you don't feel obligated to say that.

Amina Blacksher: Really, you threw us into the deep end with your studio. There was this pressure to develop and become an expert at an architectural language by the end of the semester. You needed to create your own formal language with software that you had likely never opened before and by the end of the semester, you were going to be presenting your thesis on that formal language. That was pivotal in terms of having to become an expert at

Discussion with
Mitch McEwen and **Amina Blacksher**

something. There's value in struggling to expand your toolkit and pushing through things like additional tutorials. In a way, that experience followed a law student model; the student might not know something, but they are taught to know how to find out. That experience gave me the confidence that I could figure out anything, and it was really pivotal in terms of my capabilities. Zaha Hadid is someone that I hold up as a role model, as she not only came from a background of math and painting, but she also was always an outlier who just leaned into everything. At Yale, she always taught her studio during semesters I couldn't take it, but I admired her resolve and tenacity. I see the sacrifice that it took. I should also mention Gordon Kipping as a mentor. I worked for him for a little over a year before applying to graduate school, and then worked for him again afterwards.

Mark Foster Gage: I also know Gordon Kipping as he taught for several years at Yale with Frank Gehry. When I started teaching studio with Frank Gehry there was some overlap there. We also both had practices in the Lower East Side. Look at that, we both have a connection with Gordon—Clearly, all roads lead to Yale.

Amina Blacksher: And you both won the new practices citation from the AIA.

Mark Foster Gage: This is true. Mitch, you're bound to end up at Yale sooner or later.

V. Mitch McEwen: I'm just fine right here.

Mark Foster Gage: You were both impacted by your various teachers quite a bit. Have you similarly been impacted now that you're both teaching?

Amina Blacksher: Teaching for the past five years has provided the experience of being able to articulate and put forth a position succinctly. I was often the most junior person in these settings and there were people there who had taught me or had been on my juries. Having to then put forth intelligent rhetoric and not dial down what I was thinking, even though it might be contesting their ideas, has provided valuable experience. I'm also influenced by our newly merged practice. I don't have an undergraduate degree in architecture—I studied dance and pre-law—so I've always seen form as dynamic and changing over time. This partnership has been a useful way of tethering that thinking, and a great back and forth of complementary strengths.

V. Mitch McEwen: I'm so glad we're doing this because I didn't know that you don't have an undergraduate degree in architecture, Amina. That means both of us didn't do an architectural undergrad then. When I started architecture, I was more focused on martial arts than I was on architecture. I was constantly leaving the studio to go downtown to do capoeira. I would go to Brazil and do these weeklong events

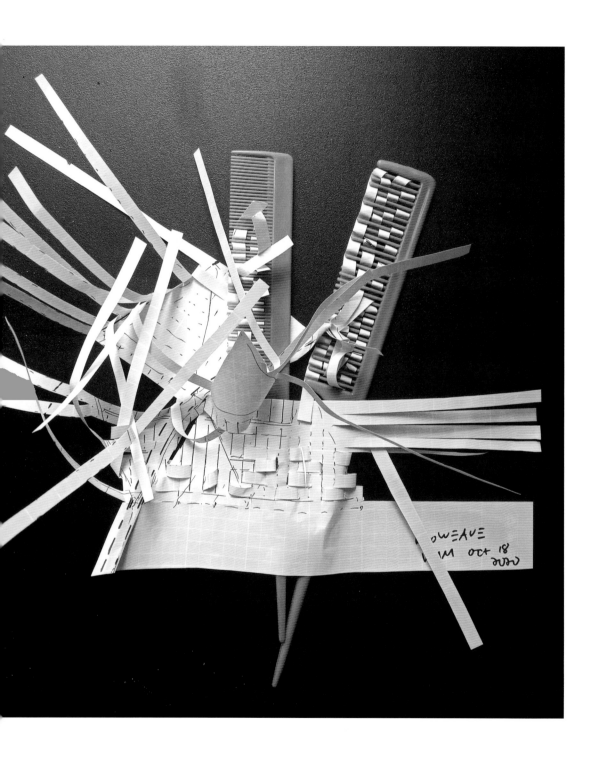

OWEAVE IN oct 18 2020

Discussion with
Mitch McEwen and **Amina Blacksher**

where we would perform. I was serious about architecture, but I was at least equally serious about capoeira and a little bit of Muay Thai as well as some cross training with MMA. It really wasn't until I worked at Bernard Tschumi's office that I started to focus on architecture more specifically.

Mark Foster Gage: MMA…I will make a point not to disagree with you during this discussion.

V. Mitch McEwen: It's been a long time since I was serious about any of these martial arts because now, unfortunately, I'm serious about architecture. That said it really was those ten years that shaped me more than any architectural mentorship. Specifically to architecture, my current boss and the dean at Princeton University, Mónica Ponce de León, is not so much a mentor as someone who just puts me places, like some Greek half-deity. She changes me by just putting me in a situation that's going to transform what it is that I do, from robotics at Michigan to the embodied computation lab at Princeton. She tries to tell me certain things that I should do for my career and usually I politely tell her that I'm not going to listen to her, and I just keep making decisions on my own. That almost doesn't really matter because the situations that she sets up for me become the situations that impact me.

Mark Foster Gage: I think those are the best types of mentors, not necessarily people who tell you what to be or tell you how to be, but just give you opportunities to let you become yourself. You might have very different architectural ideas, but Mónica has clearly been a supporter of you from when you were at the University of Michigan to Princeton University. Robert A. M. Stern has been a person like that for me. We don't agree on a lot about architecture, but he did open a couple of key doors that ended up really influencing my life in significant ways; The same is true with Greg Lynn. But I'm curious about the relationship you had with your capoeira master, and how that helped define who you are now, because that's a new one to me in an architectural discussion.

V. Mitch McEwen: Pretty much everything I do architecturally is from capoeira. To give one example, there is this distinction that is so common in the discipline between complexity and the everyday, or between theory and practice. In capoeira you don't call it sparring; you call it playing capoeira because capoeira is a game. It's a kind of colloquial idea in West African warrior practices that then had to be hidden when folks were enslaved and brought to Brazil. These practices in West Africa do not distinguish between playing and fighting, and between dancing and kicking. It's all continuous and there's music in their songs. In the West, people see capoeira and they think, "Oh, you're doing break dance," but it's flipped; break dance came from capoeira and Brazilians in New York in the '70s. People tend to think, "Oh, you're not really fighting." I did taekwondo and karate and other martial arts before I came to capoeira, and in most martial arts when you're sparring with somebody you hit them lightly; this is your sparring partner so you can't be knocking them out. It's not boxing, right? You can't be knocking their head all the time. What you end up seeing is that black belts in other martial arts that I knew on the west coast would have this problem, where they're so used to pulling their kicks that when somebody is actually attacking them, they pull that kick. I don't want to train myself that way; I want to train myself to kick all the way, all the time. What that means is that the opposing fighter must evade.

Mark Foster Gage: That's super interesting, and the idea of playing full-tilt architectural theory and practice as a combined thing is compelling. It's certainly the reverse of what the trend has been in architecture's recent history, as the PhD military industrial complex focuses on theory, or more accurately theories of history that have very little to do with practice today. It took me a decade to figure out how my own theoretical writing was informing my design work. When I did my first book on aesthetic theory, people thought I was nuts because they didn't know what those ideas had to do with architecture. Everyone was still into Deleuze. Now I'd say, and

not because of me, that much of contemporary discourse in architecture is dominated by discussions of aesthetics. This is the same in philosophy in the work of people like Jacques Rancière. For architecture, they're much closer to practical application than ambiguous differentiations about becoming with ideas you would find in Deleuze. That would make a great book: *Architectural Theory: Capoeira vs. Deleuze*. We'll split the royalties.

Amina Blacksher: I just spent three months in Brazil living in a house of all women capoeira teachers and I didn't know that you started with that background Mitch.

Mark Foster Gage: This is turning into a couple's therapy session with all that you're discovering about each other. I'll be billing accordingly and will shortly be asking you both about your mothers.

Vivian Wu: How did you come to learn the business side of architectural practice and what would you recommend that we do if we want to start our own business?

V. Mitch McEwen: One of the things that drew me to architecture was that it's one of the few fields where a firm of fifty people is still fairly common. When you look at law or business fields you see massive consolidation and a much larger organization. I came from a technology and finance background on the west coast into architecture

partially because I like the business model, which is a little perverse because architects are always complaining about money and not knowing how to make it. We spent months focusing on our business plan. One of the reasons architects don't make money is because if you're looking at the traditional delivery of documents there are very few building types that are particularly profitable; museums, towers, and airports. We have our eye on a museum first, a tower second, and I don't know if we'll ever get to airports. We have a stack on our desk for client outreach that will lead us first to museums.

Amina Blacksher: We decided early on to work on getting to the starting point of our practice as a design exercise. There's a way of taking precedent and figuring out what you can glean from other practices and then deciding what profile and what kind of practice you want to have. It's a process of mixing and matching to define a profile for you. This means you need to become fluent in how you're going to make money and what kind of clients you're going to target. That creativity is something that we've taken on, and it speaks to that panoramic approach of our studio.

Mark Foster Gage: That's an important aspect of practice that nobody ever tells you, that it takes effort to get to the part where you even start designing. There's somehow this idea that architects get paid

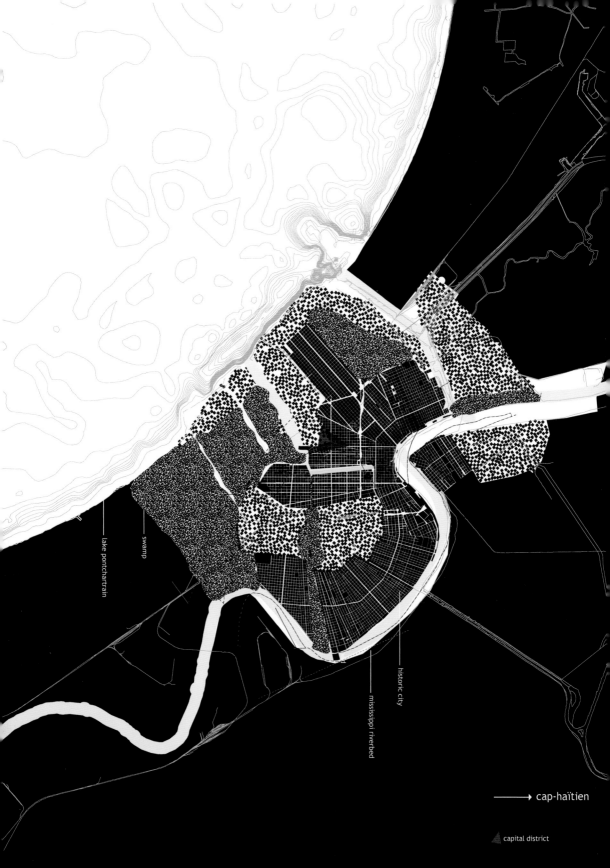

lake pontchartrain

swamp

mississippi riverbed

historic city

→ cap-haïtien

▲ capital district

to design and we do all the other stuff like client meetings, determining parameters, and figuring out the program, for free. I learned most of what I know, which isn't necessarily a lot, about how to run a practice from Frank Gehry. I never worked for him but did teach in a studio with him. I would give him rides back and forth between Yale and New York, so it was kind of a "Tuesdays-with-Morrie" thing. He has very clear ideas about which clients he takes on, what they're going to pay him, and he spoke in a very kind way about it all. What I learned is that it's not going to get you anywhere to be a "prima donna," although he of all people certainly would have the right to be. Instead, if a client couldn't meet a budget he'd just rather honestly say, "Oh, I would really love to do this project for you. You have such an interesting organization and it's been such a pleasure to meet you. I just can't run my office and do this type of work for that budget, but I really wish you the best." Of course, they'd always find the money. I started doing something only ten years into my practice, which addresses the work that goes into a project before you really start designing, or even meeting. I put into place a "project opening fee." It's not a deposit, you don't get it back, and I'm not going to apply it to future billings. It's a way of saying, "You have to pay a certain amount of money up front to establish our commitment to each other, and what that gets you is that I open up a folder, I put a

couple of people on the project, I introduce you to them, I tell you about our process, I get your information, etc." You need to get paid for that stuff otherwise you're just hemorrhaging money until you get to design. Then when you get to design, the more time you spend on design the less money you make—It's the architect's worst kept secret. Everything we teach you how to do well in school is design, but the truth is that if you want to make a profit in architecture you want to get your design time down to zero. There's a real conflict there and you two are right on the money with this upfront understanding that you need to get paid for a lot of the things that architects don't ever even think about getting paid for.

Amina Blacksher: Part of it is also educating the client, the extent of which depends on whether they have worked with

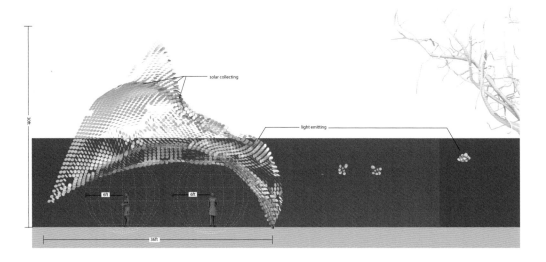

other architects before. Before you get to any sort of design conversation there is this preemptive period. A firm I used to work at would call it "visioning," and that involves a ton of work. It's like a client orientation, getting them to know that the work you're doing is designing the process of design, and that there is this responsibility that you take on in order to allow design to happen. A lot of clients may not be familiar with that process, and if they are, there is still some familiarization that needs to happen with your particular practice methods.

V. Mitch McEwen: Mark Wigley, who was formerly the dean at Columbia University when I was there, also had a significant impact on me. One of the things that he talked about was designing the client. Designing the client is a kind of strategic work, shaping them by changing their perspectives about architecture.

Sydney Maubert: I am interested in Amina's jump-rope robot from the Black Imagination Matters event. I wonder if you could speak about your line of thinking for that project.

Amina Blacksher: I am not an expert in robotics, so this conference was an opportunity for me to have access to these tools and have a platform to discuss the research. I had dabbled with a few projects using the giant KUKA robotic arm at Yale, but other than that I didn't have much experience. As for the conceptual side, the way I thought about the body in that project comes from Kyra Gaunt's book, *The Games Black Girls Play*; it explores embodied formulas that we have in our body that record and understand, to a high degree, complex relationships. Things like the trip reflex that keeps us from falling, or proprioception, a concept that I think about a lot, which is certain awareness about parts of your body's

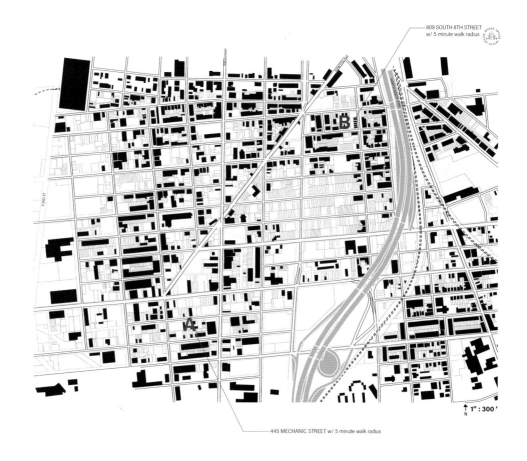

809 SOUTH 8TH STREET
w/ 5 minute walk radius

445 MECHANIC STREET w/ 5 minute walk radius

1" : 300'

extremities; you can clap your hands over your head without having to look at your hands because you know where they are in space. There's so much knowledge in the real three-dimensional space that we live in, and in our experience with buildings and our bodies, but we design in a computer with no gravity or thickness. The question then becomes how we take that intelligence from the real world and see it through the digital process. In architecture we use drawings where signs and symbols represent things, but the actual space and consumption of design is in the real act of visiting spaces, with the body, physically. This project was trying to take coordination from an analog intelligence, and feed that into a digital system. We were trying to teach robots, known for their precision and ability to repeat a task an unlimited number of times without tiring, the sophistication of rhythm and synchronicity that is integral to syncopation in hand-clapping games. The question became, can this really smart machine understand "Miss Mary Mack Mack Mack" in the same way

Discussion with
Mitch McEwen and **Amina Blacksher**

that a five-year-old girl can. Surprisingly, some of it is not so simple and the project was trying to unpack some of that complexity and intelligence. One of the broader themes that this project falls under is in uncovering certain biases in machine learning algorithms that are based on the humans that teach them.

Mark Foster Gage: Your experiment with those robots shows that certain ideas don't necessarily need to result in how to make a building. Just the act of trying to feed this set of information, of jump-roping, into a robot is an experiment that you can learn architectural things from. Those certain things might produce other certain things that might end up becoming ideas you can implement in architecture. We need to get away from the idea that all experiments need to be something you can directly apply to a studio or office problem. That's what I appreciated about this project. It's an example of this urge to explore something that just seems weird and interesting. We deal with space. We deal with choreography. To my knowledge no one in the history of architecture has ever thought, "We should look at the patterns of play in five-year-old black girls." It's such an interesting new set of intelligences that you bring to the table and into the discourse.

Amina Blacksher: I get that question a lot, "How is this architecture?" This has absolute relevance and application into how we engage with machines spatially. It

has absolute relevance in terms of tracking motion in space. I look forward to it as an ongoing conversation, not necessarily in any iteration of this specific project, but it's a prototype for many different forms of looking at processes for design.

V. Mitch McEwen: It's also really challenging this western assumption of the discipline as visual. It never made sense to me that architecture exists as a visual discipline. To me, thinking of architecture as a proprioceptive discipline is just the starting point. It's not even radical or challenging anything. It's bizarre to think of architecture as a visual field. The fact that there's 400 or 500 years of work based on this bizarre idea to me doesn't make it any more normative, it just makes it dominant but bizarre.

Mark Foster Gage: Mitch, can you talk a little bit about how you developed the idea of the Black Imagination Matters Symposium. What was the catalyst that made you think, "I really want to explore this set of ideas." Also, what surprised you that came out of it that you didn't expect?

V. Mitch McEwen: It started with the critique of not only the presumptions of the discipline but also how that bakes itself into our tools. I was actually trying to think of Building Information Modeling, or BIM, outside of the way that we typically think of it. Get rid of everything that you think of in terms of knowing software like Revit and just think of those ideas as territories to explore. The collaboration that got the ball rolling was with Nijah Cunningham, who was a fellow at Princeton University at the time. There was this desire to collaborate based on an exhibit that Nijah had curated from the collections of the Princeton University Art Museum. It was a stellar exhibit, and it was really the first time I got close to a Howardena Pindell painting. Anyway, there were Basquiats and there were Kara Walker paintings, pretty much any brilliant black artist you can think of, Nijah had put together in the show. But the show had really emphasized paper, and something about the paperness of the work made me want to think about BIM, and then it just kind of spiraled from there. More recently, part of what was generative from the BIM incubator was Adrienne Brown's book called *The Black Skyscraper*. She was also looking at W. E. B Dubois, specifically with his science fiction short stories. Dubois has also been a really influential figure for me. From data portraits to science fiction to social surveys, he was always moving in a way that I understand as being obsessed with bodily information and bodily speculation. In a way, Dubois is a kind of proprioceptive social scientist, which then immediately pushes you into science fiction.

Elise Limon: I wonder if you could talk a bit about how you reconcile working through these very theoretical concepts with a more bodily understanding of moving through the discipline. My second question is what was both of your first teaching positions and how did they come about?

V. Mitch McEwen: Well, the answer to the first question is you just do it. I'm thinking about one of the things that my capoeira master said this morning. You have a belt in capoeira, but it's called the cord because it comes from a string. He would say, "The cord doesn't play for you." And what that means is that you can have all the titles you want, you can have the awards, you can have the status, you can have the office, but if you're not designing, at some point you're not going to be a designer. The status doesn't design for you, the award doesn't design for you, and the cord doesn't play for you. You have to do the things in order to do them.

Mark Foster Gage: When you started teaching, how did that impact the way you thought about your practice and your work?

Amina Blacksher: Deborah Berke had a big impact on me in my first year of teaching at Yale. I remember her telling me to claim the space, get my name up, get my website up there, claim the space even if it's just a couple model shots that represent projects. Then, having the expectation to develop my pedagogy drove me further. It took that first year to consolidate

everything I had done over the past decade and get it together as my work. Ariane Lourie Harrison was always telling me to write my manifesto before I graduate, and now I pass that on to the students. You need to know what you're about by the time you finish your M.Arch so that then when you go work for other offices you know what critical thing drives you.

Mark Foster Gage: Hearing you talk about your interest of merging the physical with the digital, and the importance of real forces like gravity on the body is resonating with me because I was on your website earlier this week and saw that you have your project from the advanced studio in 2010 on it. To put this in context, Amina's interest in that studio was doing an architectural project that used gravity to deform cloth. In retrospect, that interest in gravity and physical realness to space was an interest you had in our studio even back then, and you are still working with it now. I hadn't thought about this connection before now. You were trying to program the computer to use gravity to deform cloth realistically, rather than letting the form of your project behave abstractly in this weird gray background environment where there's no force. That interest in gravity, weight and the body are things that I see carrying through all the way to what you're doing today. It's interesting because I don't think, as a student, you would have said, "My name's Amina, and my architectural focus is all about gravity, weight, and the body." Yet, there was a precursor seed of it back then. It's my dream for all of my students to develop their own precursor seeds in their studios they take with me; that they develop something that they later

Discussion with
Mitch McEwen and **Amina Blacksher**

realize was the formation of what might become a lifelong interest or something of value to their design practice.

Amina Blacksher: I'm so glad that you made that connection. I hadn't realized it. I was thinking about form as dynamic in how forces acted on it as a mass. I love how this interview is unpacking things. We've done interviews together before, but I think this is the most extended, with the most questions and detail. So, this has really been a chance to be in dialogue with ourselves too.

Mark Foster Gage: What is it like being a black woman in a profession that, painfully, has almost no history of including such voices in its canon or operational lore?

Amina Blacksher: Our existence is resistance. I've been in so many settings where I'm the only black woman in a firm or in a student body, so it's something I'm just accustomed to. I wouldn't be able to survive if I didn't know who I was through my history, through my black history, and through my African history. Understanding how I am here today is a necessity for me to have any agency to create. There is a way in which just showing up is revolutionary, and so, whether you say it or not our existence is resistance. I grew up in a world that said, "You are not human," or "You don't belong." I'm grateful for what has actually been given to me, like the will to get things done and put my voice out there and to create. As we said before, the impossible is just the beginning.

V. Mitch McEwen: We are an unapologetically black office. Even before January 6, roughly two years ago, I wrote about these white power symbols that would crop up on Getty Images. Images of folks doing this "okay" sign, and the "two" sign. These are white power symbols, homophobic patriarchal symbols; They're also just "okay" and "two." I've written about how this banality can serve as trafficking, as a way of enabling, in the way that Keller Easterling talks about the superbug spread. The banality plays a part in the spreading of the semiotics and practices of white supremacy and hatred; Lawns operate in the same way and pitched roofs operate in the same way. Of course, the difficulty lies in the fact that you can't just ban the "okay" sign. We can't just constantly work with binary, rather, we have to be very astute and very sensitive. As architects we're not necessarily trained that way. We are trained to be astute when we're not being sensitive, and to be sensitive when we're not being astute. An example of this is the community planning meetings where you don't really care about design; Everybody's using magic markers and bad paper, and they're just making big circles on things. This is sensitive, but it's not astute. We have to change our positionality. We have to work on weird stuff and we have to be unapologetic with weird stuff.

Third Chapter

Oddkins, Hybrids, and Philosophies of Practice

Discussion with
Ferda Kolatan
of SU11 Architecture + Design

oddkins, affinities and hybrids, pure organization versus fluidity and ambiguity, planarity in relation to 3D space, generative history versus teleological history, origins and style in hybrids

Mark Foster Gage: My interest in conducting these interviews is to sample the landscape of architectural discourse today and explore how various architects are engaging with it. Of the architects I am interviewing, your contributions to the field have been particularly interesting in their formal registers, which I know emerge from some ideas you have about historic objects and oddities.

Ferda Kolatan: In order to frame my design research, it would be helpful to build out a definition of hybridity in architecture today, starting with the main characteristic of a hybrid; broadly speaking hybrids oppose the type of ideology that believes in purity. When you trace architectural history, you will notice that there are phases that privilege ideologies of purity and there are phases where these distinctions are broken down or challenged. There is something continuous about this lineage, not as a cycle, but as an oscillation between two very human tendencies. One tendency is to seek a clearly identifiable purpose, with everything centering around a single idea. The second is an impulse to rid a culture of such a single set of notions by trying to find new ways of expressing diversity and hybridization. Clearly, I am on the side of hybridity. I am also interested in the history of our relationship with hybrids and trying to identify how and why certain eras are more interested in hybridity. I recently wrote an article that addresses the 18th-century concept of Rocaille, which epitomizes such a movement away from a larger, singular, universal understanding of the world.

Mark Foster Gage: You see this type of tension in the arts as well, where Clement Greenberg's claim to an absolute flatness of the canvas in a Manet, becomes polarized against abstract expressionist artists like Jackson Pollock, Mark Rothko, and especially Helen Frankenthaler. On the other hand, hybrid interests begin to question that paradigm through a heightened interest in art production and art objects. Hybridity becomes central to artists like Eva Hesse, who challenged the need for the canvas with materials never before used in the arts.

Ferda Kolatan: Joan Fontcuberta is an artist I've been really interested in, and his work also falls within that same subversive territory—addressing issues of human perception. More recently than that, I have been obsessed with these miniature Turkish paintings. Native to Turkey, my parents moved to Germany before I was born. Having grown up with a strong Turkish culture, there is something I find very interesting about these miniature paintings. They originate from Persian art, however, the Ottoman Turks also deployed a similar

technique, creating millions of these miniatures. The paintings are very small, maybe six to eight inches tall, and they depict a diverse range of categories; battle scenes, everyday life in the palace, everyday life in the city, erotic scenes, etc. The ones that I am interested in are those that work with architecture. These scenes display an interesting disregard of perspective, more accurately, a disregard of the correct Renaissance style of perspective. There are distortions of space and a total flattening of the surface that brings everything to the foreground, effectively removing the background from the painting; Everything is equally important, everything is equally detailed, everything is equally there for us to use in some potential way, there is no fall-off. I love that idea.

Mark Foster Gage: You can see that same idea present itself in Pre-Raphaelite painting, where artists like Rosetti would paint a single leaf with the same attention and level of detail as a person's face. The philosopher Timothy Morton calls this "ecological art," describing expressionist art in the same way; The artist does not relegate "nature" to the background where it receives less attention than a foregrounded human subject, the artist renders both with equal attention. Understanding both Turkish miniature and Pre-Raphaelite painting as tools for flattening and questioning constructed value systems, these mediums are particularly salient given the increasing importance of diversity and equality in creative practices.

Ferda Kolatan: This idea also finds its way into how I work, how I design, and how I teach; Similarly, there is no fall-off. In every little detail that we show of an architectural design, there is something that is being developed to a very high degree. I am also interested in the relationship between planarity—in the two-dimensional, scenographic quality of space—versus architecture's three-dimensional quality. Our work explores how these qualities interact with each other in a hybridized manner. This exchange offers moments where one of these conditions begins to fall to the background for the other condition to occur. We are interested in the legibility of each formal cue that informs

the hybridized object, if the end product outwardly speaks the language of the miniature, or if it becomes something that has lost the obvious markers of its origin.

Discussion with
Ferda Kolatan

Mark Foster Gage: I want to know how you were formed as an architect, how you picked up that interest in history and art, how you were shaped, and who you were shaped by. Did you have any specific mentors? You've crafted this unusual interest in avant-garde areas of technology, a discourse in philosophy, and a real deep-rooted

interest in history. How did you bring these ideas together in your work?

Ferda Kolatan: I went to a technical university in Germany to study architecture for six years and then attended graduate school at Columbia. During that time, one of my studio courses was taught by Greg Lynn. He never took much interest in my work because I wasn't quite getting it right at the time, however, my time in his studio significantly impacted my architectural sensibilities. I was very interested in what was being taught, but it was quite a break from my architectural background in Germany. He would ask us to work with geometries that, having attended a rather straightforward technical University, seemed completely outside of the realm of architecture. It was not easy for me to design in this way, but it entirely changed my perception of contemporary architecture. I began to understand a distinction between contemporaneity and modernism that I hadn't previously learned. Modernism is a particular ideology, and something that started and ended during a specific period of time.

Discussion with
Ferda Kolatan

Mark Foster Gage: Greg Lynn taught at Yale for the first seventeen years of the 21st century. Having spent the last twenty years at Yale myself, as both a student and an instructor, he had an incredible influence on my development as well. I taught seven advanced studios with Greg during that time, continuing to develop a discourse interested in the expanding influence of topology and technology in architecture. Coming from a technical university, did you pick up the technology easily?

Ferda Kolatan: I developed an interest in technology, but not in an innate techie way. I am honestly not a technologically inclined person, but I was able to address that work in an aesthetic way. I learned how technology can bring entirely new languages into design, which is riveting. My process always starts with the aesthetic. My design work doesn't begin with the intention to do something meaningful, it starts with the search for something interesting. Once I find it interesting, I ask why it could be meaningful.

Mark Foster Gage: That search that you describe extends to the use of history as well. Perhaps his technical work overshadows his knowledge of history and precedent, but I found Greg Lynn studios always have that element to them as well. It's something I related to, having preceded my teaching years with an entirely classical program at Notre Dame and a year

living in Rome. How did history enter your box of discursive interests?

Ferda Kolatan: During my education, I had no real interest in history; I was more interested in what you, I, and a handful of the other architects were doing with technology. We shared a path together in developing many of the ideas that today are considered to be part of the historic digital project. Eventually, we began to see the limitations of that particular project and started to open it up to all different kinds of influences. In my own case, that's when history started to creep in. There was a moment in time, around 2010, where I was

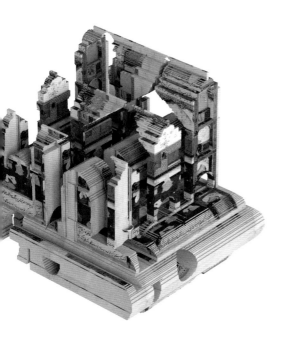

invited to produce a project for the Turkish Biennale. I started working on it in 2011 and that was the first moment where I thought, "I don't want this to be only digital." I became interested in what would later be called a post-digital mentality. At the time I described this as "digital crafts," forcing myself to include elements into my design work that didn't come from the abstraction of digital spaces within software. I didn't want to start with a surface, I didn't want to start with five NURBS, I didn't want to start with anything that was loaded with a certain protocol. This may not sound like a big deal, but I remember I was stressed out at the time because for so long I believed that was the way

to create novelty. I realized how difficult it was to bring history into the computer. Once I did, however, an entirely new world opened for my design work. I remember the excitement I got from this realization. The project did not look old, or postmodern, or any of the fears that I had when I was bringing in history. More importantly, it did not look like a digital surface. It looked truly strange, and I was completely satisfied with what I wanted. I started to include this fusion of historic architecture and digital modeling in my teaching. I taught a series of studios that were based in Cairo, then several more based in Istanbul, both with very strong historic architectural traditions. I asked the students to closely study the type of architecture, art, and material logic that those places had developed over time, to look at the characteristics they were known for. After that, they were to hybridize their findings with technological componentry or ideas from some other kind of aesthetic device.

Mark Foster Gage: In a way, history became your muse.

Ferda Kolatan: It started with the initial belief that history did not have any role to play. It was easy to view history through a teleological lens; it was that which brought us here, rather than something generative. History was simply important knowledge if you want to be a well-educated person. I reached a point where it became more useful than that, and it's actually something

I see in your work quite a bit as well, Mark. The work foregrounds history. We understand that some kind of causality no longer exists in the same way we thought it did, and it's not taught in the same way either. Ten or fifteen years ago if you wanted to understand Palladio, you would actually study what Palladio did; his first project, his last project, his mentor's, etc. Today you just type it in, and you get a lot of images. There is something scary about that, but there's also something interesting about it. It speaks to how we register knowledge and what knowledge means for us. There's a radical transformation happening across society, where knowledge is becoming something different than it was even twenty years ago.

Mark Foster Gage: How we access history is different and therefore our idea about what history is, and what it produced, is also different. This is the fallout of learning about Palladio through a few books, versus doing a Google search and seeing 100 images of his work come up with varying degrees of applicability and redundancy. Granted, the Google search is also showing much more information than you can get from a book. It is neither good nor bad, just different. You get a much higher quantity of information but the chance it's wrong is that much greater.

Ferda Kolatan: This new type of understanding also impacts our values and how we assess good design, now and historically. It impacts how we might read into some kind of causal heritage, or how we understand precedent. None of these judgements work the same now as they did twenty years ago because all of the information is at your fingertips, but its accuracy is highly varied. History then becomes a revitalized tool, used in an entirely new way. This era of information describes an interaction with history that doesn't fall under a slavish historicism, or a postmodern understanding of history. This isn't putting a temple on top of a high-rise; It's much more deep-seated in the reality we are inhabiting. We have no origins anymore, neither in terms of time nor in terms of place. How then do we design in a world like that?

Mark Foster Gage: One reason I put you and Michael Young adjacent to each other in these interviews, is that although you speak about it differently, there's an important role that fiction takes in both of your works. To continue the Palladio analogy, you describe this change in the nature of historic knowledge, and how a Google search on Palladio might give you a couple hundred images. That search might be sprinkling four or five images that are actually by Scamozzi, rather than Palladio, and these images still get included into your head as a constructed truth about Palladio. It's not necessarily a nefarious pollution of fiction, but the fact of the matter is that fiction exists in the vast quantities of

knowledge that we now have access to and consume. There's "fiction powder" interspersed in what we believe to be our historic knowledge, and I think you and Michael are working with these subjects in your individual projects. Given all of this, tell me about your practice and understanding of discourse now, at this exact moment. What other disciplines are you looking at? Who are you absorbing right now? Who are you channeling? Who are you reading? Who are you in dialogue with?

Ferda Kolatan: When it comes to the role of fiction there are a couple of names that are not new, but all still quite relevant. Bruno Latour is an ongoing influence on me. He gives us the mother definition of hybridity in regard to modern society as far as I'm concerned. Latour describes modernity as a hybrid in itself, beginning with humanism and the Renaissance, characterized by what he identifies as a split-personality between objectified nature on one hand and humans and cultures on the other. Latour eloquently connects this linkage between modernism and the enlightenment, to questions of technology and objectivity; the modern belief held that if something was scientific and based on fact,

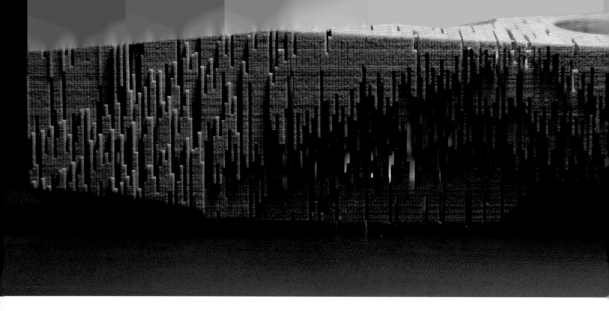

it qualified as real. Latour is a master at exposing the holes in this argument. In *We Have Never Been Modern* he describes this value system based on the "technologically informed," "scientific," or "objective," as simply contingent on the machines we build as extensions of our point of view of the world. There's always a bias, and that bias can also be understood as some kind of fiction.

Mark Foster Gage: Interestingly, Michael Young uses fiction through the art practices of parafictionality, while you unpack fiction as something embedded in what we understand to be the truth. You can clearly see something being addressed within multiple disciplines simultaneously. It allows

Discussion with
Ferda Kolatan

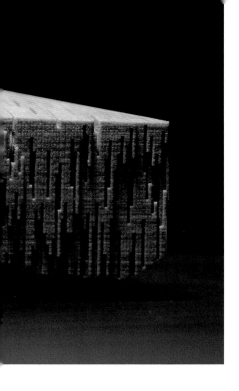

you to very easily have cross-disciplinary conversations about these topics, but it's also a sign that you're onto something that's clearly in the ether and relevant.

Ferda Kolatan: My brain lit up when I read Latour for the first time. Up to that point, I hadn't questioned a reality based on scientific objectivity. It should be made clear that I'm not a science denier, however, Latour's writing helps us understand that there's a fictional aspect to the things we call facts at any particular given moment. What you do with that information is up to you.

Mark Foster Gage: How does this understanding of fiction impact your design work?

Ferda Kolatan: While the discourse came from Latour, I also discovered artists that work along similar lines. Again, Joan Fontcuberta being the most explicit. He is a photographer and artist who builds exhibitions around certain topics that are completely fictitious yet built with incredible accuracy. That's the brilliant thing, you understand them as real. His work puts you in the space of not quite knowing and you're left to pick up on traces that seem odd. That engagement with the "real" is something that we always have to be alert to, challenging and poking at; the need for this turning of the mirror has been accentuated by recent politics. People like Fontcuberta and Latour get accused of using fiction to deliberately mystify, when in reality, it produces the exact opposite effect; fiction becomes a form of emancipation, a way of understanding that there is also tyranny in the way our current information systems portray scientific notions. Similarly, Donna Haraway is another theorist who is very influential in my work. Her *Cyborg Manifesto* is a brilliant text and it can be easily expanded into other disciplines as well. She argues that women have been obviously defined by male patriarchy over centuries and her solution is, rather than pushing back, to embrace this weird hybridization and find authenticity in it. You can start to depart from there and begin to think about it in architectural terms.

Mark Foster Gage: She's asking us to renegotiate authenticity, to begin to define

reality by a weirdness rather than a push for purity. Women's rights have been defined by patriarchy. When we fight for women's rights, to ignore this patriarchal influence is to ignore the truth.

Ferda Kolatan: It's a break from a dominant, Hegelian, understanding of evolution. Haraway's writing is positioned against constant dialectic, against thesis and antithesis, etc. She encourages us to understand that the hybrid holds value in itself. In her recent book, *Staying with The Trouble*, she makes a very similar argument in ecological terms. Though her work on an Anthropocentric and Capitalcentric discourse is less oriented to feminism, she describes a link between all of these ideas. Her ecological argument is similarly against the notion of "going into the streets" and trying to turn the clock back. First of all, that would be futile. In a lot of ways, it's too late, so let's not be stupid. Instead, she sees this situation, albeit challenging and problematic, as the condition in which we need to operate. One of the terms she coins in this book is "oddkin," which I've rented from her many times in my teaching. I've specifically been working with a concept that I've termed "oddkin architecture," based on a similar interest in composite conditions and the hybrid as a thing in itself. I'm experimenting with ways that architecture might embrace these tensions, rather than treating them as something that

Discussion with
Ferda Kolatan

can be resolved positively or negatively further down the road.

Mark Foster Gage: One aspect of teaching that I've become particularly interested in, is the possibility for students to develop an awareness of those moments that you described. It was a lightbulb moment when you came into contact with Greg Lynn or when you read Donna Haraway. These powerful moments fascinate me. We all have unique touchpoints; certain people, texts, or ideas impact us as architects who hold an interest in dialogue and discourse. It's interesting to hear how they so dramatically influenced certain trajectories. My general theory on education is that you never learn consistently from everything you come in contact with. As a student, you ignore 95% of what you come in contact with in school, but that remaining 5% knocks your socks off and that determines who you're going to be as a designer operating in the world.

Elise Limon: Do you see your work being political? I get a sense through your interest in Latour and Haraway that you might. Can you expand upon that?

Ferda Kolatan: Firstly, a political stance is unavoidable. There is nothing that you can produce and put into the world that is not contingent on material forces, on capital forces, on institutional forces, on who I am through my own history. Before we design anything, we are designed by our

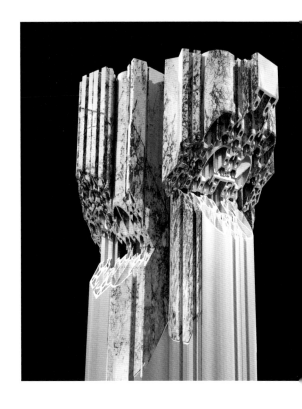

countries, institutions, and cultural norms. So, there is no way for any architect to operate apolitically. The question becomes, do you embrace an overtly political message in your work? Are you aware of it yourself, or are you clueless about it? My answer is that I avoid any kind of overt political messaging through my work. This is, again, very different from not being political. I would describe myself as a very political person, but I don't want my architecture to be read along a direct line toward a particular political message. I don't think such singular political messaging aligns

with my interest in hybridization or "odd-kins." I do not enjoy art like that. I love art and I spend a lot of time looking at art and visiting art installations, but art that exists as pure messaging, to me, becomes something else. Many people hold the opinion that no matter what you do, if there is a certain kind of injustice in the world that is being clearly defined, everybody needs to prioritize and address that particular injustice in their own work. That is an impossible task. We need to have the freedom to understand when and how architecture becomes meaningful, and how we, as architects, define that meaningfulness. For instance, I know there's a military regime in Egypt and I know it's problematic, yet we still chose to enter an architectural competition in Egypt. I still chose to bring my students to Egypt to study the culture of Cairo. Cities provide a political milieu within which you act, but it's more subtle, more diverse, and more layered. I have a planetary attitude toward politics when I consider the Anthropocene, which is an easier problem to address from a design point of view; It's not easy to solve, it's just easier to address. Other kinds of political questions reside in different realms, and I think we have to be very careful with what we believe we have to contribute to those problems.

Mark Foster Gage: We all wish that political engagement through architecture was linear and causal—that it operated like a call-and-response effect. We've all seen various design studios and architectural projects, in school and in the profession, that follow those beats, "There's a refu-gee crisis, and architects need to address the refugee crisis immediately, and this is how we solve the refugee crisis through designing shipping container housing and putting people on cruise ships. Our work is done here." In reality, the refugee crisis is a hyperobject, introduced into philoso-phy by Timothy Morton as an object that is too vastly dispersed in space and time to be fully captured, or perceived, by the human mind. The global and local forces that perpetuate certain phenomena are beyond human comprehension. Turning a shipping container into refugee housing isn't a solution to a political problem, not to mention the fact that they would all ef-fectively become ovens—Architects tend to ignore that cruise ships are massive heat conductors. I think you're right in noting that architecture can operate on multiple ontological levels, and I think it operates on multiple political levels as well. It's very rare that architecture operates directly on specific moments where an injustice is identified and then fixed by architecture.

Saba Salekfard: I was reading about the AI Studio Prize you received and your "Real Fictions" Cairo project, and I noticed that it called on students to present their ideas as decontextualized objects. Here is a quote, "Rather than suggest specific solu-tions, there is a need to present prototypes that could be presented at different scales." How does that idea influence the way you

approach different projects in your prac-tice. How do you navigate from objects, to spaces, to buildings?

Ferda Kolatan: When I took my students to Cairo, we visited sites and we went to lectures focused on building preservation, all organized by a government agency, al-though I'm clearly not a preservationist. We also met individual groups and archi-tects who work in Cairo, and we imme-diately realized we landed along a battle frontier of different interests. It was highly politicized. We met with one group who told us not to meet with the other group; we met with another group who didn't want to talk with us because we had talked to the first group. If you know anything about the history of Egypt, looking to Arab Spring and further back along very similar trajectories, it is a place with an increased concern for life and death matters. If archi-tecture wants to be critically active it has to engage people who live in places like Cairo, where there is a very different set of concerns to what we have in New York,

New Haven, or Philadelphia. This is of course nothing new, but it hadn't dawned on me to such a high degree until I went there. I realized that it wasn't going to be a studio where we can just make a nice little design somewhere and put it in a corner in Cairo. It all felt so utterly meaningless to me at that given moment, and yet, that was our original plan. I had picked a couple of sites we would visit, we would split the students into teams, and they would find solutions for local problems. After a couple of initial meetings, I brought all my students together and I said, "Sorry if this is coming out of the left field but forget the syllabus. We're going to completely restructure this. This is not going to work." The students were great, they felt the same way.

Mark Foster Gage: So, this gave you a way of working on architecture and political problems without necessarily choosing a side. As a studio traveling from New York and Philadelphia, this is also slightly tactical because you always run the risk of producing work that falls into the white American saviorism category. The "prototype" idea offers a solution that can then be adapted by those who are actually "on the ground" so to speak. It's more sensitive than developing a single, inherently uninformed, top-down idea from the outside.

Ferda Kolatan: This idea to decontextualize was a means for us to take the project out of the heat of this particular context, where four very different constituencies

were fighting over how the site should be developed. Decontextualization provided a type of space in which we could think about solutions that might not be super local, however, they were absolutely driven by ideas that are particular to the place. I want to be clear that this is not a process that rejects local information. Rather, it's about rejecting the notion that anything within a locale can only be understood within the functions of its local network of connections.

Mark Foster Gage: Decontextualization continues that hybrid methodology, defining a "space" where the universal and the local can coexist. The design evades both international style and critical regionalism.

Ferda Kolatan: Is the world governed by universal principles or by local principles? This is another long-standing question within architectural discourse. Modernism is all about universals, a claim that "We're all the same. Everybody's going to love white buildings with flat roofs and pilotis." We eventually discovered that people don't love such uniform modernism; in fact, they usually hate it. People over here hate it, people over there hate it less, but they all kind of hate it and they all have different reasons for hating it. That said, I believe that we can share ideas to address larger groups of people than just local areas. I would hate the notion that we just have to go back into some kind of medieval mindset where we all work in one particular

village of ideas, and everything outside of that village is the enemy, so to speak. I do believe that there is a middle ground where we can talk globally about certain sets of ideas and then bring in specificity and locality. The prototype might be one such solution.

Vicky Achnani: Your work is divided between academic research and your practice. How do you approach a project with ideas that have been formed by your academic research when it's driven by a specific client-driven brief? How do you incorporate the ideas like "hybridity" and "oddkins" into your real projects?

Ferda Kolatan: I graduated from Columbia in the spring of 1995, and I started teaching that following fall. Since then, I haven't gone a single semester without teaching—this includes most summers.

My point is that it's impossible for me to take the academic research out of who I am and how I approach design. However, I learned to speak to different constituents by trial and error. I speak differently to clients than to my students. I present work differently to a committee for an award, or for a submission, than I do for a competition. Over time, you learn how to determine what resonates with the audience that you're speaking to. This layered approach between research, teaching, and clients is built into the practice.

Mark Foster Gage: I think that's important to note. There's so often this underlying assumption, especially in architectural schools that you have one concept, and that concept is your building. End of story. So, you learn to visually diagram the concept to show the direct relationship between the concept and the building.

I think architecture operates, as I've said a million times, on multiple ontological levels. That is to say that architecture operates in many different states of being. It operates at the level of function, it operates at the level of political engagement with its context (whether or not the architect intended it that way), it operates at the level of sustainability, aesthetics, etc. It can't, and shouldn't, be whittled down to a single thing, although that certainly makes it more consumable. One-liner architecture might net more money or build more things, but you're not producing architecture that's of any cultural value or service to our communities or humanity. This reminds me of a Ferran Adrià interview I was reading where he talks about this revelation he had when he was looking at a tomato; no one ever really uses the seeds, we just throw them away so we can use the harder, redder parts of the tomato. He realized when he scooped out the seeds that he had this wonderful tomato gelatin product that surrounds and protects the seeds, which he started using in his dishes. This description or process doesn't appear on the menu. He doesn't jump out of the kitchen and tell everyone who eats that tomato gelatin how it came to be. People eat it, it's delicious, and they consume it without knowing the story. Sometimes he tells the story, sometimes the story is written down in a book, sometimes it just tastes great and you don't need to know the story. The culinary arts have no problem operating on multiple ontological levels. For whatever reason, architecture has come to champion the idea that you need one concept or idea that's so clear that you can diagram it with big arrows, feed that to your professor or client, and you're a genius. Architecture doesn't need to infantilize itself like this.

Taiga Taba: Recently Peter Eisenman taught a studio at Yale about hybridity. The guy that explains architecture through dialectics was making the case for hybridity as a way of creating a third space,

Discussion with
Ferda Kolatan

something new. Does hybridity always have to be referential? When I look at your chunk models, if we call that hybridity, do we always have to be able to identify each element of the hybrid or do you think hybridity can be something that's self-referential or maybe even non referential.

Ferda Kolatan: There needs to be a recognition of something else. There needs to be a reference that is legible. I call it an "echo," meaning it can be recognizable, but weakened in its recognizability. I don't work with abstraction, at least not in this phase of my life. I like things to come in with histories, with references, although I accept that those are often fictional in some sense or another. Just to make things clear, I am not interested in the discourse of dialectics. You can't believe in dialectics and then reject some kind of teleology of history, because they are intrinsically connected to each other. The hybrid is interesting to me as an artifact, as a kaleidoscopic thing. It is not a stepping stone toward a better place, it is not a tool to break something and therefore to rebuild it in a better way.

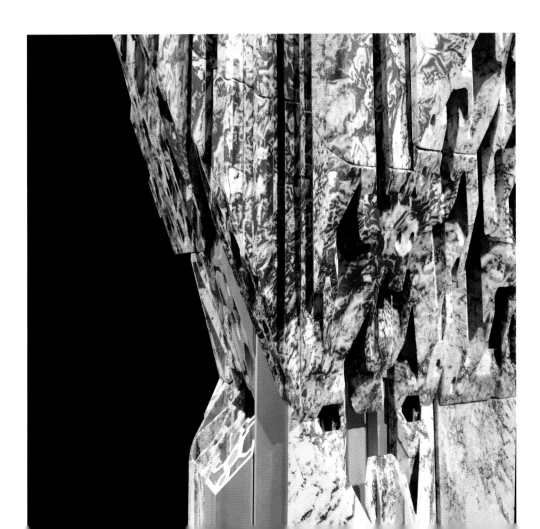

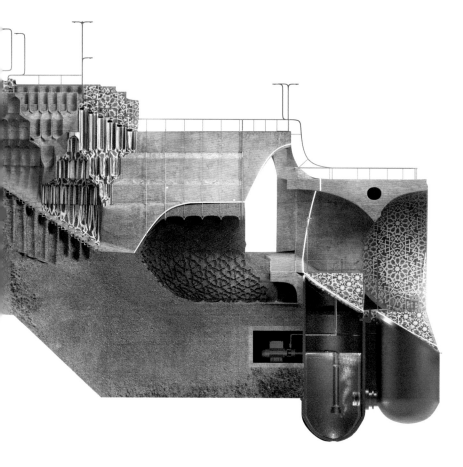

It is an existing condition that we usually recognize as inferior and try to fix, and I don't want to fix it. I want to make this ambiguity and this tension better and more interesting. I want to alert people to it. That's how I look at it. So yes, to me it's important that there's some kind of legible reference.

Taiga Taba: Maybe the reason Peter brought the term hybridity and third space into the studio was because he thought that the world had become too complicated to explain everything through dialectics.

Mark Foster Gage: It's funny how Peter always has a way, similar to Philip Johnson, of knowing what the newest topic in architecture is, but he always insists he's addressing it in a special Peter-only way and not in the same manner as the groups discussing it. At one point Michael Young and Peter were both teaching a studio on the subject of aggregation in architecture, and I remember hearing Peter say to Michael, "Yeah, but your aggregating isn't the same as my aggregation." I would suspect that Ferda's hybridization isn't the same as Peter's hybridization…

Discussion with
Ferda Kolatan

Ferda Kolatan: I was just listening to him lecture rather recently. When I listen, I often totally agree with everything he says, and then when I see how he designs, it's a very different way of working. He says one thing but what he means is something else, and he almost always ends up developing a universal modernist project. Of course, he doesn't see it that way. He talks about Palladio and his treatment of a portico as an act of hybridization, for instance. When Palladio pushes the portico into the facade of the building, to him, that is a hybrid. That, for me, is too subtle. I need more closely put together references. It doesn't make my hybrids more valid or less valid than his, but it's an interesting observation.

Young Joon Yun: When you hybridize different objects, do you believe that a new style or articulation should be generated?

Ferda Kolatan: It goes without saying, and it's the same for anyone who does work like we do that we hope what we produce is new and different. To claim otherwise would be absurd. When we talk about "oddkin" relationships and hybridization, I'm certainly interested in finding or driving toward a condition where, in the largest context, I can define as some sort of style. That said, style is very problematic, it's a word loaded with all kinds of other issues, and I wouldn't necessarily say that I believe in it. Style is no longer the right word in the context of today's non-authentic, non-original output of work. It relies on some continued coherent set of parameters that allow us to look at something and identify what belongs to a certain genre. I don't think we can do that anymore, but we can certainly produce projects that have an affinity. That's another word I use a lot.

Mark Foster Gage: Naturally, the issue of style sends you right back to that problem of purity. For instance, there are plenty of things that are and are not in the International style. So, if you're talking about styles, you're also talking about a way to identify purity. There's an irony in thinking about a hybrid style because the two definitions are diametrically opposed.

Ferda Kolatan: I agree, but it's also true that people look at the work that we do, and the work my students do, and they recognize it rather quickly and easily. There's a signature buried in the work. On one hand, I do like that. Years of thinking and research went into this work and of course, I want some kind of recognizable quality of that work to survive in the world. I think its familiarity allows it to go on to create some kind of impact. However, if it immediately melts into the mainstream as merely a new style, you would not achieve that. As Mark said, style immediately tries to set a boundary; you're either in or you're out. Style becomes a new kind of universalism, and that is fundamentally against the idea of hybridity.

Fourth Chapter

Earth Protectors and Mega-Component Construction

Discussion with
Tom Wiscombe
of Tom Wiscombe Architecture

tinkering versus inventing, railing against minimalism, happy accidents, pro-effort and anti-one-liners, mentors versus manifestos

Mark Foster Gage: I used to have this worry as a young architect trying to engage with architectural discourse and innovation that my work, and the work of all of my peers with similar interests, was always only going to appear in books and magazines and never quite get to the real world. I take pleasure in the fact that you're building so much and helping me get rid of this worry. There's something interesting in your work that goes beyond the work itself. Most architects think, "I'm going to design this innovative thing, here's the plan, sections, and elevations and this is the person that will build it." You've been flipping that script in a way. You've developed this tendency to go back to the underlying operating system of architecture and tinker with it. You are questioning why we create plans, sections, elevations. You're interested in why our sections always erase the identity of our buildings. To take that analogy further, most architects are playing with different software, while you're changing from Linux to Windows to IOS and hacking things at this sub level before you even get to questions of architectural form. There's an interest in interrogating how the profession operates, and the way you talk about your work is interesting because it's so cohesive. You talk, not about a section, but about a "Godzilla" and a "tesseract" and "shears" and you're challenging the structure of both representation

78

Discussion with
Tom Wiscombe

and discourse through those ideas. You're challenging tectonics when you talk about the mystery in how things are put together rather than the structure or the skin. And while those two elements aren't necessarily established, it's something that you figure out for every project. That's not really how the profession works, but it's how you seem to work. How did you learn to dovetail all of this into your practice?

Tom Wiscombe: I want to start by saying that you are one of the most outspoken and clearest thinkers of our generation. It's really nice to have you take a minute and think about what the hell I'm doing. You're right, I'm literally trying to strip it all away. It's an intuitive process where I just don't like something in the world, and it becomes a target. I love that you see it as hacking the operating system of architecture, I'm going to use that! A big part of my hubris when it comes to building comes from my time with Wolf Prix when I was working as his senior designer at Coop Himmelb(L)au, which was a dream. He is fearless and he let me take the biggest risks. I remember when we did the BMW World project's contract for construction. I managed to slide some amazing features into the final agreement, including what I call radiant structure, which meant that all of the primary and secondary profiles were hollow and filled with water and argon gas. Yes, we ran radiant in the floors, but we also did in the structure, like a giant 3D radiator. Without that, we never could have satisfied the German energy regulations. We also stuffed the sprinklers inside the hollows to make them go away. BMW was very happy, it reminded them of car design. At Wolf's office you could dream up anything and they always leaned in.

Mark Foster Gage: It sounds like figuring out a puzzle, not just doing CDs and turning them over to a contractor and answering a couple questions. It's more like inventing than it is building.

Tom Wiscombe: Yes inventing, that's a good way to describe it. I'm interested in theory and I'm interested in how things get made in the office, like many architects. So it's in my nature to deep dive all the way down through representation, but also through how you build something. I do this

because I'm interested in addressing systemic problems, hierarchies, and architecture's limits. I will say, part of it also has to do with the fact that I simply don't like being told by others what can and can't be done. I just don't really trust nay-sayers. My experience is that you can do absolutely anything you can think of.

Mark Foster Gage: There must have been a moment when you were in Austria working for Wolf, where you had been for a decade, and you made a decision to move to LA and start your own teaching, work, and practice. It was a big risk, but I suspect that it was lucky for you that you landed like little baby Moses in a basket at SCI-Arc's shores. SCI-Arc has a lot of like-minded people who think of architecture in terms of innovation rather than established professional protocols. How did you find the people that thought like you, and how did they continue to influence your work after that initial contact and experience with Wolf? How did you establish an architectural family of peers and did this influence your work?

Tom Wiscombe: I was just leaving Los Angeles to go back to Europe when Hernán Díaz Alonso and Marcelo Spina came to SCI-Arc in 2001. So, I missed the first few years when SCI-Arc was reinvented by the then-younger generation. However, when I came back to LA several years later, Hernán and Marcelo and a few other people had started to build new

Fourth Chapter
Earth Protectors and Mega-Component Construction   81

repertoires through new digital tools and started thinking about the issues that these tools consequently created. They had legions of followers, which was a different experience. It was super exciting to plug into that in 2006. Peter Testa had just come over from MIT with Devyn Weiser. It really was a great family at that time. And one cannot leave out Jeff Kipnis, who was both marauding around the school gunning for us all through theory and also making us stronger in the process. Teaching at SCI-Arc at that time was really about live discourse, and my practice was about doing competitions for real projects.

Mark Foster Gage: You wanted your friends to win, but not really.

Tom Wiscombe: Not really. Second place max! But yes, it was an awesome time and I wish that a little bit more of the younger

faculty at SCI-Arc had that sense of empowerment and fearlessness. We all actually thought we could win! Now I'm seeing some cool and outrageous ideas that are just being left on the table, with no hope of building. This is probably due to the fact that competitions as a means to win and build is defunct. They're an outdated mode of practice, and although Wolf was able to do it, it's no longer a viable way to run a practice. Even if that is the case, competitions still provide a forum for live discourse out in the world. It was a way of just trying things out, trying things on, and seeing how my peers approached things. That ended up being super productive.

Mark Foster Gage: There was a formative period where a lot of architects were starting their careers and using new digital technologies, and a lot of the work looked a little similar because we were all trying to figure things out with the same software tools; there was a commonality to the work. So when I was flipping through your new monograph, I was searching for the moment when "Tom became Tom." In the book, you state: "We're not deforming. We're glancing. We're not finessing, we're throwing it down, etc." From my perspective, it took you some time to figure out that do/don't list I'm sure, which seems like it was your way of declaring a break from this uniformity between those early digital projects. It was a way of saying, "I'm not doing it the same way everyone used to be doing it, I've found my own stuff and this is what I'm calling it. I'm not doing your drawings anymore. I'm doing Godzilla drawings. I'm not doing deforming and pushing and pulling control vertices in a software program. I'm doing slicing and glancing blows," and so on. It made me realize, "Oh, Tom's all grown up." He's got his own language and his own techniques. It felt very declarative and

I could see all of those things from the first list were the things that everyone else was doing, whereas the things in the second list were things that only Tom is doing. It was a really interesting moment for me to see. If Botticelli had painted it, it would have been called *The Birth of the Architect*.

Tom Wiscombe: I appreciate that. It's funny to have arrived at something so simple like that list and take a lifetime to

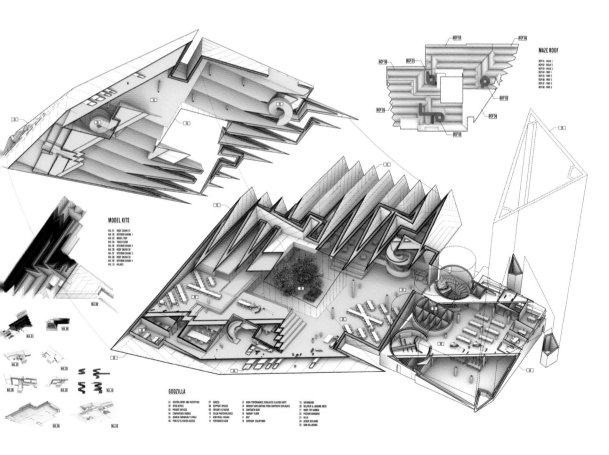

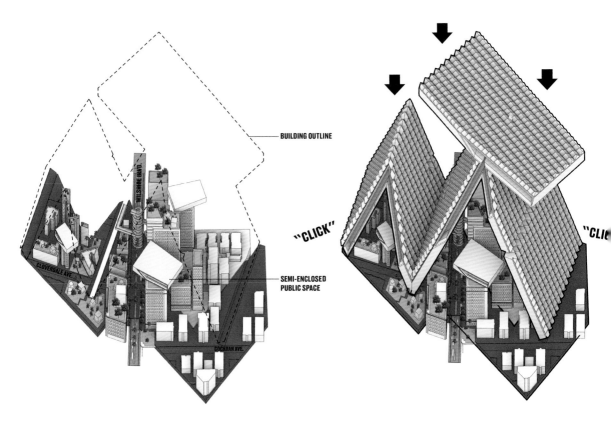

BUILDING OUTLINE

SEMI-ENCLOSED
PUBLIC SPACE

"CLICK"

"CLIC

get there. I'm still not even there, really, but it does feel at least like I can be more focused now, and like there is solid ground beneath my feet.

Vicky Achnani: You describe models as the primary tool that you use, because of the model's ability to bridge the gap between the design and reality. Can you elaborate more on the tension that takes place in the translation of the model into built reality?

Tom Wiscombe: When you build something full-scale out of metal and it's all welded, and it looks very serious, it's always kind of funny to me because all I'm seeing is the smaller model blown up. We invented a language of super components by having cheap 3D printers. So, a limitation in what the 3D printer could print in terms of size, forced us to make 3D models out of several smaller chunks. This translated to a way of thinking about the project at full-scale, where it is similarly built in relatively smaller chunks. So the 3D printed plastic model became an architectural construction idea. Sometimes you have to go out of the system to make a discovery, and drag it back in. I'm interested in the way that really dumb, playful, or even obvious things can be literalized at the full scale, so that full scale stops being so serious and it doesn't take the life out of the model. A lot of things we build with are the shape and size that they are because one or two humans have to carry them across a construction site; bricks, sticks, panels, logs, etc. I'm continually trying to get rid of these traces of industry.

Mark Foster Gage: I wasn't aware that the idea of those giant panels coming together came from a limitation of 3D printing, and the inability to do what you want in the scale model. We seem to never speak about happy accidents in architecture, but they're hugely important in the history of architectural innovation. Things like penicillin, post-its, and the microwave being used as an oven were happy accidents, so we know this is an aspect of design that exists. We should be more attuned and aware of this as architects.

Tom Wiscombe: What's interesting is that the components of the model, when they're scaled up into full-size construction, are really strong structurally because of their interlocking shapes. Another happy accident. You first sense it when making the physical model, friction fitting almost holds the whole thing together.

Mark Foster Gage: Well the architectural default for construction is, unfortunately,

to push around programmatic boxes a bit, then buy 4x8 panels of an insured facade system and stick it on a grid that can be applied to your boxes. Architecture is becoming a commodity built with default software and products and it's surprising how many great ideas come simply from not accepting the system that you've been given.

Tom Wiscombe: It's so true. If you go to architects' offices who are very serious, they'll have these amazing material sample rooms and they think having such

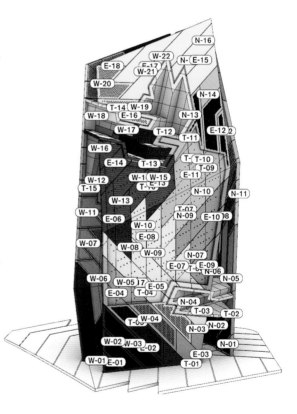

a large collection of materials is showing possibilities, but for me it's showing limitations. You're basically just a decorator at that point, a selector of materials and samples. When you go "shopping" in the material library it's just another form of mass consumption. If you're trying to be inventive in architecture, everything needs to be invented.

Mark Foster Gage: Pushing boxes around in BIM with drag-and-drop materials might be the death knell of the profession, pushing it over the line into commodity status. It's already happening now; architectural projects are awarded not for innovation as much as for those who pushed around the boxes in the most interesting way. There must be more for the future of the built world than confusing innovation with pushing around boxes. A city filled with voxel-buildings is a depressing thought…

Samar Halloum: Considering the consistent language across your work, does your approach to design change when the scale of your project changes? Also, do you recall certain misconceptions that people have about your projects?

Tom Wiscombe: Architecture itself, as a thing in the world, has to be enough. It has to be something that you encounter, and you connect with independently of any ideas that underwrite it. We can never stand next to our buildings like docents from a museum to explain where the ideas came from. I think it has to exist on its own terms and at the same time. However, I also think there's a second life that projects have, which is in their history, precedents, influences, and concepts, interesting maybe only to experts. That's what we do in academics. We spend a lot of time trying to figure out that second life at the expense of the first. To your first question, I love scaling things wrong. Scaling things up and down is very powerful and it's one of my favorite techniques to design with. As Mark was saying before, we all used to use these super-complex tools and series of operations. This idea of "digital virtuosity" admittedly produced some timely work, but I'm more interested in the primitive and rough digital translations.

Mark Foster Gage: I think there's a near-universal reaction against the smooth and abstract continuity of the early "digital project" in architecture. Your recipe list that I referred to earlier seems to be your way out of that previous genre of work.

Tom Wiscombe: Right now, I'm interested in jamming things together, scaling them up, and making copies. Move and rotate are amazing too! This is not me looking for the "easy," but it's the only way to make things that I find interesting. Things that are too slick or smooth aren't interesting to me anymore. Industrial design did it better, and it killed that thread in architecture.

Discussion with
Tom Wiscombe

Mark Foster Gage: Agreed. The iPhone is celebrated for design when it's essentially defined by its lack of design. Every year it gets more minimal, and this is always confused with better design. This is a problem today, that design is confused with something having less features. If you can't see a button or a camera lens, it's a "good" design. You can already see a universal snap back against this, and eventually, there will be more reversion. I won't be surprised if, in the following few decades, you start to get smartphones with stamped sculptural relief on the back. Minimalism renders things seamless and invisible, rather than making them have character,

cultural value, or, I dare say, beauty. I don't think anyone's iPhone 11 is going to become a cherished family heirloom. Making things featureless and minimal just makes them more disposable. It's what corporations want, for you to throw things away and buy more. So, we don't value our phones, or our cars, or our furniture—because it doesn't have design, it simply has the absence of features.

Tom Wiscombe: We made a desk one time and just used an old competition project upside-down and scaled down by 10,000%. It was for our Kinmen Port Terminal entry, the one with five rotating

Discussion with
Tom Wiscombe

mega-jack shapes. It's the same game that Rem Koolhaas played when he recycled the Y2K House design for the Casa de Musica project in Portugal; He just scaled the former up to become the latter, which made him realize, "Oh wait the stairs don't work when it's ten times bigger." I like that kind of problem because it makes you rethink everything.

Mark Foster Gage: On the topic of misreading your work, I remember speaking at a symposium vaguely on the subject of post-digital thought and these architects, younger than you and I, were talking about your work. One of them said something like, "Yeah that guy Tom Wiscombe tries way too hard," as if it was a bad thing to spend too much time on design and care about it too much. I remember that being such a foreign idea to me, the idea that you can spend too much time on design, and now people see that as a bad thing. I think of spending extra time on design as a way of valuing a thing, wanting it to have more of a cultural presence in the world. I love to design in the same way a pianist loves to play the piano. If you don't like the piano, why become a pianist? If you don't like to design, why become a designer?

Tom Wiscombe: When you spend a lot of time working on things that don't get built, you have a lot of pent-up ideas that you want to execute. So, you tend to pack a lot of stuff into a single project, maybe too much. My Sunset Spectacular project

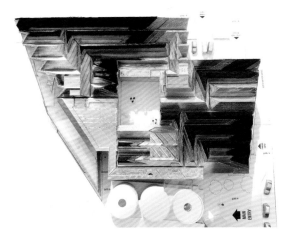

probably suffers from that. If I were to redo it today, four years later, I would take away half of its features. Making something look easy is actually the hardest thing to do! I find the anti-design "lifestyle" mantra really infantile. Look around for ten hot seconds and tell me who is out there making a difference in the world with that lackadaisical approach. No One. Long term, it's a losing proposition, one I don't wish on that generation.

Mark Foster Gage: This attitude doesn't take into account the fact that design can be enjoyable, and that this isn't a choice between being lackadaisical and working 90 hours a week in an architecture firm. I design in my head when I'm driving. I design when I'm at dinner and someone's droning on. I design when I'm walking my dogs.

Tom Wiscombe: What does easy architecture really mean anyway? It made sense when Robert Somol wrote about it in 2002, positioning it against the complexity of form, but now it seems like plain old laziness! You just start repeating what is in front of you in the world and you find people who agree that the repeat is good enough. It's not like that for me. It's our job to push boundaries. Architects are one of the few actors in the world that can actually suspend reality, and through it provoke these big philosophical questions. We create large objects that humanity has to deal with. We have an ethical responsibility to push. Architecture always levels some kind of critique on society with whatever we do, and that's a good thing. People change over time, too. I'm 51 and I operate differently now than ten years ago when I was doing twelve competitions a year. I'm not doing that now. Now I'm carefully thinking about business development and trying to figure out how I can level up, do larger projects, meet different kinds of clients and really help them. It's not just about me anymore. I want to work with people where I can make a difference, beyond my own personal aesthetic interests. I'm working on a new project with that same solar developer that I worked with for the Dark Chalet, and this project actually really helps his business. It's exciting for me in an ecological sense but it also requires a level of invention, and that's the new kind of ground that I want

Discussion with
Tom Wiscombe

to be in. I'm performing more now for a different audience than just my peers. This was totally different ten years ago, when we were all primarily focused on performing for one another.

Mark Foster Gage: That's a good observation. I often ask my students, especially in studios, what are your motivations for doing that design move you just did? Are you trying to impress me? Are you trying to impress your peers? Are you really interested in that material? Are you doing it because no one else in the studio is doing it? Investigating the motivations that make you do particular things is something that I only just started doing. I realized how useful that would have been if I had been asking myself that when I was a student. If I had thought, you know, what's my

motivation for this? Am I just desperate to impress my instructor? Half the time that was probably the case. Was I showing off for my friends, or I was trying to get a scholarship? Am I really interested in what I'm actually doing? Architects need to unearth the arcana of why they do what they are doing.

Tom Wiscombe: That value statement is so important, today more than ever. What is it about? How is it more than just your private self-serving project?

Saba Salekfard: I saw you speak in 2014 about tattoos, the problem of subdivisions, and the role of contamination and precedent. Here we are, a few years later, talking about flat ontology and object relationships. How do you evolve and expand on

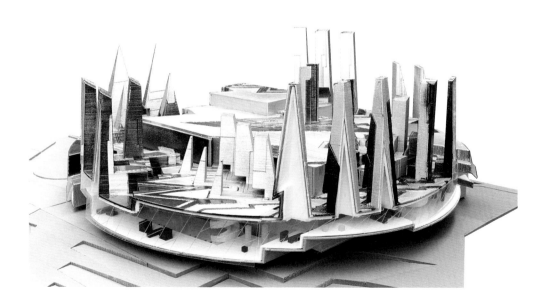

your work? My second question was about your role in teaching. What is the responsibility of educators now with this new generation of students?

Tom Wiscombe: Yes the "Status of Subdivisions" lecture was my way of introducing the architectural audience to the idea that there is an actual alternative part-to-whole thinking, where the whole is greater than the sum of the parts, and the

Discussion with
Tom Wiscombe

things inside other things, can exist equally. The flat ontology. The tattoo is one of the best examples of a flat ontology of architectural parts, where the ornament, which is always downstream from the mass, is set right next to the mass, and they dance in a loose and equal way; Neither one is subjugated by the other. The other question you were asking was about teaching. I taught at SCI-Arc when Neil Denari was the director, and then it was Eric Owen Moss, and now it's Hernán Díaz Alonso. Quite frankly I don't think that's had a huge impact on what I'm working on. It definitely sets the tone for the school, there's absolutely no question that those are three really different people. Neil brought the ideas of precision and design culture into the school, which was great for me, because I feel like I am a similar animal. Moss was really focused on the intellectual life of the architect on the one hand, but also "the hunk of concrete" out of which architecture is ultimately made. Hernán has been focused on communications and expanding the field of architecture, but now the defining feature of his directorship, and of all of our programs, is really taking a hard look at the social and environmental state of the world, especially vis-à-vis diversity. The work we have done this year has been important, and I'm proud of it. I'm currently obsessed with what I call the "Flat Out Large," building parts that are tiny in one dimension and massive in the other two. Like giant playing cards, that can

whole is a unity. I was reading about this idea of a strange mereology at the time from Levi Bryant, and that was a eureka moment for me. That discourse described all things as parts and that all things, even

lean on one another over swaths of a city. They create vast, protected, shaded spaces as a way of caring for the city. I think of them like Godzilla, earth protector: kind to humans but also vexing and alien.

Mark Foster Gage: These mega-proposals of giant urban solar playing cards that shade a large part of a city are interesting in that you can put one anywhere, they have a generic aspect, but certainly when you put one down, it's entirely site-specific, and not reconfigurable. It's an innovation on the typical "specific" versus "reconfigurable" argument in architecture. The reconfigurable could be represented by Louis Kahn's British Art Center, where the whole building is very configurable; you can move any wall. It's like playing a musical instrument. Conversely, the super-specific is represented in the work of Frank Lloyd Wright, who will design the toilet paper holder exactly far enough from the toilet so he knows you'll have to stretch. He designs every little aspect of the design of his project. You can't change anything in a Frank Lloyd Wright house or something else falls down. Your Godzilla earth-protector playing cards are both, but only by virtue of their scale.

Tom Wiscombe: I'm so interested in that. We have this shorthand around the office that describes the amount of design a particular project can support. If we are really leaning on it and it's going to be a position piece, it might be 50/50. That means,

50% is for the discipline and the other 50% we'll figure out how to make it work. I'm now more interested in the 90/10, which is essentially something that's going to be much more straightforward, with a few special features. This doesn't mean 90% functional, what it means is 90% familiarity. I'm convinced that human needs are incredibly flexible, and that we can make anything work functionally. It's much harder to get people on board with something aesthetically unfamiliar.

Mark Foster Gage: Frank Gehry talks about his projects like that as well, as in how much "Frank Gehry-ness" can you afford. When I taught a studio with Frank I remember him using those terms. He was describing the winery he was working on at the time, and when they presented him with the budget he basically told them they could afford a certain percentage of their building to be "Frank Gehry." The rest was just going to be bland, or at least straightforward. The best example I think of this is his project for Bard College where this beautiful "Frank Gehry" facade sits in front of simple beige EIFS boxes. He's very clear about the balance between the unfamiliar design language and the economic viability and function of a project. He juggles them better than just about anyone.

Tom Wiscombe: Yeah, he's super smart that way. Although I'd probably use "background" instead of bland, because there can

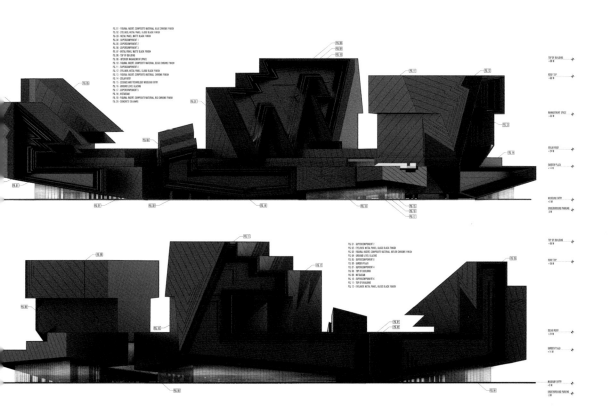

be a lot of mystery and intrigue in backgrounds as well. My favorite project of his is the DZ Bank in Berlin for that reason. That's like 95% box, 5% "Frank Gehry," which is this insane "horse's head" conference room in the main atrium/courtyard. It's a great diagram for architects to work from. I'm trying to do it, but it's difficult when you have a bunch of stuff pent up that you want to get out on the table. We all have limited time on this planet.

Mark Foster Gage: Rem Koolhaas said it best when he said any architect basically has seven buildings in them. How are you going to spend your time? Are you going to spend your time taking on those ten-bathroom renovations or are you going to spend that time and go after one project that you might not get? What are you going to do with your seven buildings? You got two under your belt Tom. Five left.

Tom Wiscombe: No, those are both starter projects. I don't know what the first one is going to be yet. I guess the word architectural "practice" is perfect, because you practice getting better with each building.

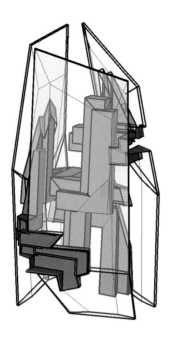
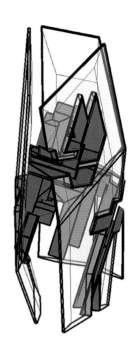

Mark Foster Gage: Is there any work that you're doing now that developed as an idea when you were a student? Are there any slow growing, long term ideas still present?

Tom Wiscombe: Yes, I recently showed the final project from my grad school work at UCLA to some SCI-Arc thesis students actually. I told them, this is so old, I don't know what to make of it. It was a casino in an empty lot in Vegas, based on a vast space filled with these little cone-like objects sticking up through holes in a kind of blanket or surface. There was also a very blocky hotel box at the back, so it was a whole bunch of elements loosely tied together. I remember Greg Lynn said I was a modernist, and I wasn't sure what he meant. Looking back, I'm sure he was commenting on how I was using the composition of objects rather than what he was interested in, which was shape-shifting and families. I realized that I actually had a dose of copy-scale objects in there, which only came to define my work recently. I learned a lot from Greg Lynn and Robert Somol, in particular, their interest in the difference between shape and a more complex form. Honestly, it took me many years to push their ideas to the background and do some original work of my own. Authors curate all the time. They select. They throw out. They remember. The good news is that

the minute you start doing your own work, no matter how derivative it is at first, it still becomes your own.

Mark Foster Gage: That reminds me of a recent conversation I had with my boyfriend about self-discovery. During the course of the pandemic, I made two astounding discoveries. Apparently, I love candied ginger, and my favorite pasta is bucatini. I had no idea. These are things I never knew about myself. In the course of having time to observe things that are happening, you actually discover things about yourself. I used stupid examples, but those things happen architecturally too. You discover more about yourself as you develop and part of that is uncovering things that have been there all along.

Tom Wiscombe: You're so right. I think that's crucial. You can just run right over something you don't take time to see, and that's probably the hardest thing to avoid when everyone is so busy. We can produce all kinds of different things, but the key is knowing which one to develop. You don't get there by just arriving at it one day, you get there by making things continuously over a long period of time, trying things out. It's slow. I'm suspicious of the idea that there's this genius moment, and that you can get there without hard work and repetition. Expertise is built from time spent, not lightning bolts. Do you know that idea that expertise takes 10,000 hours of doing something, from Malcolm

Discussion with
Tom Wiscombe

Gladwell? Well, he is dead wrong. I peg it at something like 50,000 hours, at least in architecture. Whenever you deal with creative people you find out how difficult everything was and how long it took them to even be noticed, much less become famous. You can't see it from a distance. How long did Nirvana ride around in shitty busses from tiny bar to tiny bar before their sound became legendary.

Mark Foster Gage: I've been consciously tracking some of your language as you've been talking and you said you wanted your work to be magical, you wanted it to look alien, like it didn't belong there, and that you wanted it to look like it had just dropped out of the sky. These are things you want your work to do as cultural effects, but my guess is that you don't tell your clients those things. I assume you tell your clients some other stories, what are they?

Tom Wiscombe: No, not really. I am a good salesman. I can actually sell the client the ideas of the project and give them ownership of those ideas.

Mark Foster Gage: You never tell the client, "This Sunset Spectacular project is in this complicated shape because it symbolizes the complicated unity of the people of Los Angeles?"

Tom Wiscombe: No, I don't go there. I try to avoid totally separating those two ways of speaking about the project. I use some disciplinary language, but I also use everyday language when talking about context, cost, or the people involved in building it. I like to get builders and owners on board with ideas that stick, and clear language helps a lot. For instance, I'll throw the idea of a tesseract out there at a meeting, and then I'll eventually hear contractors yelling about the tesseract later on and I love it. Of course, it's a made-up word and thing, but it means something specific to all of us developing it together. Imaginary becomes real!

Mark Foster Gage: I think that's so much healthier for us as architects and for the profession than sticking easy symbolism onto buildings like Santiago Calatrava calling his transit center at ground zero, "A dove being released from the hand of a child." That's classic one-liner architecture, and it always puts a little vomit in the back of my throat. Architects shouldn't be telling people what they want to hear, or something easy to hear, they should be telling people why they're excited about what they are doing for and with them. One of my great frustrations is when an architectural object gets distilled into little diagrams. It's like a children's book that describes how the building needs sun, so then the corner is brought up to allow for sun, and the big yellow sun shoots out a big yellow arrow and boom, genius. Building done.

Discussion with
Tom Wiscombe

Tom Wiscombe: Well, I definitely do those kinds of diagrams, but it's not to explain the whole project. Those diagrams work when I'm trying to show different aspects of a project. I like projects that operate on many different levels across many different forms of representation. Good architecture isn't literal, so of course, I am also against subverting the architecture by way of overly literal diagrams. What a terrible thing to do to your work. Above all, we shouldn't infantilize our audience.

Ruins, Rubble, Recycling, and Reuse

Discussion with
Ellie Abrons and **Adam Fure**
of T+E+A+M

collapsing layers of mediation, image-objects, scenography, revealing the apparatus, non-tectonic materiality

Mark Foster Gage: I think your practice introduced some ideas into discourse that have been absent for a while, like a real interest in the way materiality is represented in both the representation and the physical work of architecture. Architects generally assume there's a one-to-one relationship between the two, but you seem to be prying open some space between those two ideas. You also have an interest in optical effects and illusions, not only to intrigue your audience but in a way that really seems relevant to the context. Lastly, you're doing what one might call "buying local," in how you're using aspects, often materials, of the site to add certain site-specificity to your work. In the art world this has been done pretty consistently throughout the ages whether it be from 60,000 years ago when humans first started rubbing ochre from nearby pits onto cave walls, or much more recently in the work of someone like Jackson Pollock who sometimes stuck his own cigarette butts into his work, or Julian Schnabel who painted on used tarps that indexed their own history. Strangely, those ideas have been significantly missing in architecture, perhaps since Kenneth Frampton was writing about critical regionalism so long ago. In your work, there is also a real interest in using models to generate real effects, instead of renderings. Considering all of these elements, I think that you are pioneering a rather interesting

combination. My first question is related to these kinds of disparate elements that you see in a T+E+A+M project. How did you coalesce as four people with four different interests? We know that you don't just commune, and ideas pop out uniformly, 25% from each of you. Whose interests became what parts of T+E+A+M? Let's start there; how did T+E+A+M happen and who brought what?

Ellie Abrons: Adam and I have known each other for a long time. We came here to Ann Arbor to teach at the University of Michigan in the Fall of 2009.

Mark Foster Gage: Did you know each other before that?

Ellie Abrons: Adam and I were married at that time, but we didn't know Thomas Moran or Meredith Miller, nor did they know each other. Meredith, Thomas, and I were teaching fellows with the University of Michigan fellowship program, where they bring in young academics and practitioners every year for a one-year teaching fellowship. That year there were five fellows, which was unusual, so we decided to collaborate. As part of this, we bought a house in Detroit for $500 as a group of five, and we each did a full-scale installation in it. Then we were invited as this sort of loose collective to reimagine that project for the Venice Biennale in 2012. By 2015, we had known each other and had been collaborating in this loose way for a few years, and the call for proposals for the US Pavilion at the Venice Biennale for 2016 was released in the summer of 2015. At that time, Adam and I had been doing this super nerdy reading group with Thomas and Meredith that was focused on the work of Emilio Ambasz, who is a favorite of ours. Mark is making a face.

Mark Foster Gage: I just remember that Emilio Ambasz used to give these lectures; he was very interested in landscape in addition to architecture, so he did half of the lecture under the name Emilio and the other half under the name Ambasz, and he pretended to be two different people. It was like watching Two-Face from Batman give a lecture about architecture and landscape. Very, well, interesting. But I love his work and ethos as well. Have you seen one of those lectures?

Ellie Abrons: No, I haven't, but I love that. We still laugh about this published interview of his, where he interviews himself and it's called "questions I asked myself."

Mark Foster Gage: When he's presenting the landscape stuff he'll say something like, "Ambasz was having a conversation with Emilio and Emilio wanted to do this, but Ambasz wanted this, so we made it out of grass."

Ellie Abrons: Yeah, I'm not surprised. We should try and watch one of those. We had

been getting together casually and talking and I think it was Adam's idea to enter this call for proposals for the US Pavilion as a foursome. We put together this proposal and we had to come up with a name very quickly and T+E+A+M came up out of nowhere. T+E+A+M being the first letters in each of our first names: Thomas Moran, Ellie Abrons, Adam Fure, and Meredith Miller.

Mark Foster Gage: It could have just as easily been M+E+A+T.

Ellie Abrons: Yeah, or M+E+T+A. We were selected so we ended up being one of 12 American practices in the US Pavilion in 2016 and that's the exhibition for which we did the Detroit reassembly plant project. At that time, we didn't know if it was a one-off or if this was going to be a thing. The experience was really incredible, and the collaboration was successful in what we wanted to get out of it, so we decided to keep going as T+E+A+M. To fill out that trajectory or to map us on a graph of now-versus-then; we're in an adolescent phase where we're transitioning these past couple of years from the speculative exhibition and gallery-based work to built projects. We're in that awkward phase where we've been working on stuff for a while, and we have projects which are supposed to break ground starting this summer. We think we know what a T+E+A+M building will be, but we haven't actually walked into one yet.

Discussion with
Ellie Abrons and **Adam Fure**

Adam Fure: I wanted to enter the proposal with Thomas and Meredith just so that we could call ourselves T+E+A+M.

Ellie Abrons: That's definitely not true...

Mark Foster Gage: You had to have a good title, above all. It's funny that around the time of that same Biennale my peers and I were all into the philosophical movement of Object Oriented Ontology, or OOO. We were all reading this work and in dialogue with the philosopher behind it, Graham Harman. So, we decided if we could get enough people together that we could be called 000-7, triple-o-seven, like 007 to the power. But there were only six people. We couldn't figure out an obvious seven, so we didn't do it. It likely would have been some terrible Frankenstein with parts from Michael Young, Tom Wiscombe, Ferda Kolatan, David Ruy, Karel Klein, and myself.

Adam Fure: At the time of that 2016 Biennale, Thomas Moran was doing a bunch of research, where he was building custom ovens to melt recycled plastic to then make new forms. That's where the material studies from the Detroit Reassembly Plant came from. Meredith Miller was writing these theoretical papers on material ecology and new ways to frame sustainability through the lens of material; where materials are, where they show up, how you can understand them in a broader sense while maintaining a tactile sense of their immediacy. This helped us think about materials in the regional way you mentioned because the proposal was for creating a site in Detroit for producing new materials from used and recycled materials.

Mark Foster Gage: Although you've been categorized as being the so-called "post-digital" group of architects, you're clearly not against the digital as much as you are against its fetishization. It seems like your work has a strong reliance on the digital, but fuses this with materiality in a pressurized way.

Adam Fure: Ellie and I have a similar background, having both been graduate students at UCLA in the mid-2000s where there was quite a bit of digital modeling going on with programs like Maya. You saw a lot of high mesh count Polygon modeling. At that time, this messy middle ground between the digital and physical has a lot to do with what we were focusing on. Fast forward to today, I think our work still falls between those lines. Thomas Moran is really helpful in thinking about the construction; he has a lot of experience detailing buildings and also just building stuff in general.

Mark Foster Gage: Thomas Moran is also a Yale graduate, notable for their material-oriented ethos.

Adam Fure: Yeah, he's a Yalie. Meredith and I grind out the design through rhino modeling, and we can lean on the group to critique our own work; everyone is involved in a kind of design critic capacity. Ellie is very much a part of that, she keeps things together on a high-level. These roles are still emerging.

Ellie Abrons: Early on with T+E+A+M, Adam and I were not only invested in thinking about the relationship between form and materiality through a formal project,

but also the relationship between the shape of a thing and the material that it's made out of, the qualities of that material, and how those two things might work together to produce some kind of visual effect that could become some kind of spatial effect. Over the years some of that has gone away, but I'm only really reflecting on that now. In other words, if the four of us began in more distinct areas, there would have been some convergence since.

Mark Foster Gage: This seems like a really compelling initial recipe: someone who's interested in physical materials that are kind of goofy and recycled, someone who's already theorizing about the eco-logical effects of such materials, and two people that have the skills to represent and manipulate those complex types of materials digitally. Again, looking back at your history, one thing that you all had in common, not as a label but as a mindset, is something I was speaking with Kristy Balliet and Jimenez Lai about in their in-terview; this idea of the "Post-digital." This mindset is loosely positioned against fetishizing the computer for all these crazy things that it can do, against digital com-plexity for the sake of digital complexity. It looks to background digital process with an urge toward reintroducing some larger ideas. In Jimenez's case, this is the idea of fun and drawing in using cartoons. In Kristy's work, it's a kind of cuteness and volume. With T+E+A+M, it's the mystery of materiality. None of these things are really being addressed by the "digital formulas" project. All of these positions were opportunities to introduce something into the discourse that wasn't there at the time. How did you end up at this point? It wasn't really in your education, considering who you worked for and who you were around in school. Those original ideas that you wanted to introduce into the profession, where did they come from? When did you know they were valuable? We all have ideas, and we dismiss 99% of them. How did you decide which ideas stuck?

Ellie Abrons: I think there's a kind of clear line between our UCLA indoctrination and the work that we do.

Mark Foster Gage: Indoctrination. That's a strong word.

Ellie Abrons: It was a pretty tight ship when we were there, but maybe that's too strong of a word.

Adam Fure: After my first year in UCLA's graduate program, I can remember writing this bit of text about the work I had completed for the student show. I remember writing that, "the digital is too white, the digital is too smooth," and trying to consider roughness and texture as something that was missing from that digital formalist project.

Mark Foster Gage: We must be telepathically connected. It was around that time

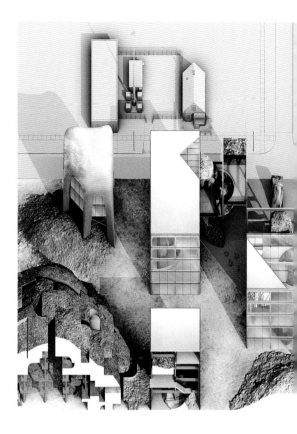

that I started to feel the same way, and the result was teaching a series of courses about the history and future of rustication in architecture; The return of texture. I've been teaching that for about seven years. You leaned into physical materials and I went to software used in the special effects industry to make things look rougher. I eventually landed on the program Mudbox, which was designed originally to put wrinkles on King Kong's face for the 2006 movie. We could have started a practice together called M+A.

Adam Fure: That was an idea in my head for a long time. When we got to the University of Michigan, Mónica Ponce de León had taken over as the dean immediately before we got there. She had transformed the culture of the school from one that was highly theoretical and representational to one that was about making. The school got a robust fabrication lab with robots and CNC machines, and there was funding to do small scale prototyping. We got to explore the overlap between the digital and the physical and these rough material qualities because we had the resources to do it through the school. It partly started as a reaction against digital smoothness, but then it became clear to us that it was a distinction that need not hold. Rather than thinking about materiality as a concept that describes an opposition between digital and physical, we were trying to understand this idea of a spectrum of materiality that moves between the digital to the physical. The barriers we place between these two poles don't need to be there anymore. That's the expanded field of materiality that we explore.

Mark Foster Gage: It's really helpful to hear you describe this moment of noticing that things like texture and materiality are missing from what you're seeing in your school, and how this absence becomes something that you embrace as a way to make an architectural project. It's not about falling in love with a faculty member, becoming an acolyte, and doing their work. It's about seeing an opportunity. I had a similar reaction when I was starting out, using all the digital technologies that you are mentioning and relating it to the rustication work. I got frustrated, around 2004 or 2005, with this relentless ambition to produce smoothness that had no complexity. Abstract supple surfaces. I just thought it was another form of minimalism and I've always been interested in figuration and complexity through detail. Although I was part of the "digital project," I was always against its underlying tendency to become a minimalist project. This frustrated me and it provided reasons as to why I got into textures, objects, and generally higher-resolution forms beyond smooth supple surfaces with no detail. That material and textural thing was missing for you, up until the 2016 Venice Biennale, and people wanted to see how those ideas might be folded back into practice. I suspect that's why Cynthia Davidson and Mónica Ponce de León, previously your dean at the University of Michigan, supported your entry to the Venice Biennale. Your work was introducing something into practice that had been missing, something that was valuable. I'm always harping on students about looking for their own opportunities to find or create their own projects in architecture. It's not always about stumbling on something, but as you noted, it could be about noticing a glaring absence. Both cases require a sensitive eye.

Discussion with
Ellie Abrons and **Adam Fure**

Adam Fure: I want to amend that statement quickly so as not to claim too much originality. We also worked closely with Jason Payne and Heather Roberge in their practice Gnuform. We were influenced by their work at that time, originally together, and later apart when they split into two offices, Hirsuta and Murmur. I worked with Jason a little bit after they started working independently. The two of them were also doing a lot of digital vacuum-formed plastic, stuffing fur in cracks, other material experiments like that. These ideas were already in the ether.

Mark Foster Gage: Modesty is the color of virtue. That's Diogenes, not me, but let's give you credit. You developed this material interest into your own ruined, rubbly, and rough architectural language.

Elise Limon: I wonder if you could speak a bit about your process in choosing the images that you're working with, in your renderings. Your work includes a lot of found imagery and photographs you've taken, and I wondered if you could speak about that process a little bit. I would also love to hear a little more about what you feel you take from Emilio Ambasz.

Ellie Abrons: There's quite a bit of site specificity in the work that we do. Not in a romantic or nostalgic way, but in approaching the site and quite literally stock-taking or making an inventory. It's a way of closely looking and observing what's there and thinking about these things as possible architectural materials. The way in which that might be instantiated or how it might be materialized can change from project to project. The Detroit reassembly plant is probably the most literal of those translations, where we actually deconstruct the building and use the old material to make a new building. It's not just in terms of physically making new buildings, but also seeing the material as an integral part of the project. The statement that the project was making was that materials have narratives, they have associations, they're not stable, and they fluctuate. These things change from person to person, but they exist. We were trying to make new images out of the same material, to put it simply. There have been other projects, for instance, the pavilion we designed, where the imagery of the site itself is printed on the building. This allows us to produce a media surface where you see a reflection of the site in real time. You

Adam Fure: Simulacrum is not an interest of ours; our work is not a commentary on how mediation is a less authentic version of the "real world." We truly believe that collapsing media, or collapsing layers of mediation into one experience, makes the image or the architecture more real. It makes the tree image printed on the glass of that pavilion more real. To have the simultaneous collapsing of an image and a physical thing, ultimately addresses how humans experience is evolving in a contemporary mediated milieu. We are trying to explore this through architecture. It's an urge to make things more real rather than less real. To answer your second question, Emilio Ambasz was working in a time when environmentalism and sustainability were emerging as interests to architecture, but he seemed to be doing it in a way that was totally bonkers and that's inspiring to us. There are plenty of ways that people talk about sustainability within architecture, but I think there are only a few people who are trying to invent new ways of conceiving architecture and inventing new environmentalisms for architecture. Ambasz was doing that in the '70s, and that work has been an inspiration for us. We are drawn to the way simple shapes come together in a balanced composition. He also works with ideas about mythmaking that have been interesting to us, how humans tell stories about the world to make sense of it. Not in the old-fashioned, exceptionalist, "primitive narrative" sense of where

experience space through reflective materials that are layered over a printed image of the site, again layered over physical objects in space. We think about this mix as a type of cinematography, where the image of the site is both reflected in the glass and printed on the glass, allowing us to play a game. It's a way of considering a multiplicity of effects as well as experiences across different times of day, experienced by different people, in different seasons, in different weather. These things would produce different images of the building, but always one which was enmeshed within its own site.

Discussion with
Ellie Abrons and **Adam Fure**

we came from, but more in how we process the complexity of the world today. It's an interest in probing for new ways in which we can evoke descriptions of the world through myths that might help us navigate our world moving forward.

Mark Foster Gage: My interest in aesthetics is largely focused on that exact concept; how reality is perceived. That's something our practices share.

Taiga Taba: You mentioned that everything could be interpreted as a spectrum of materiality. I'm interested in where your interest lies in creating alternative realities.

Adam Fure: In terms of reality or realism as an aesthetic, I think of Hal Foster's distinction between James Turrell and early Dan Flavin. On the one hand, the effect is all hidden; with Turrell, you get a cloud of pink and you don't know where it's coming from. On the other hand, you have Flavin's fluorescent tube in the corner of a room; you see the fixture, you see the plug. Foster's argument is that the Flavin is better, because you get both the phenomena and an understanding of where it's coming from. You are not duped in any way. This is as opposed to Turrell's work, which Hal Foster thinks is less successful because it just produces a spectacle that leads to the swaying of the masses. Flavin has a critical understanding of how it's produced and therefore its own experience. That's obviously the framing of a different time,

but part of our interest in exposing the glitches of software, or exposing the materials themselves, comes from that same idea that Flavin was addressing. We talk about the backside of scenography a lot. Stagecraft always has a front which is what you see in a performance, but you typically don't see the back. This is opposed to architecture, which is in the round; so as you move around an architecture with stagecraft quality, there's a more imaginable side, but then there's also a side where the materials are more exposed. That backside allows you to understand a little bit more about how the effect exists, and how the effect is produced.

Mark Foster Gage: This is where we differ in our thinking; I revel in a piece of architecture that invites curiosity. It is

better when a magician does a trick and leaves you in a state of fascination, rather than showing you how they did the trick right after doing it. I think our minds are so multi-tasked and overloaded that moments of fascination and mystery are a gift. In your case, you're partially interested in that enigmatic quality, but also in revealing the trick eventually.

Ellie Abrons: There are moments of enigma, or a kind of flickering, because we are also interested in revealing the apparatus or the artifice. When we think about a kind of spectrum of materiality, one way it becomes manifested is by breaking down any distinction between the digital and physical, both in terms of material and hierarchy. For instance, the digital object was considered, for a time, to be an idealized and more abstract version of a physical thing. The way that we work is to constantly cycle between these two poles, to take materials in and out of the computer. It doesn't really matter whether something originates through a physical material prototype or through a digital model; in the end, it's going to be a kind of hybrid, messy version of both.

Mark Foster Gage: The Enlightenment taught us to think in categories and silos. We have mammals, plants, minerals, or more specifically, taxonomic rankings like kingdom, phylum, division, class, order, family, genus, and species. This allows us to study things individually related to

Discussion with
Ellie Abrons and **Adam Fure**

similar entities, but that also has a contrary effect where we begin to separate things which may not be so separate. Your interest in this "spectrum of materiality" and the assertion that the digital and the material are not separate things is really interesting. This leads to a rich theoretical territory for getting beyond that Enlightenment obstacle to thought. I want to speak of the Enlightenment in a different way, however. This past summer and this past year have been a watershed moment for rethinking issues of social and environmental justice and how architecture engages with these subjects. Your work has been so entrenched within communities in Detroit, a laboratory for re-thinking the relationship between cities and populations that have been subject to oppression, poverty, and injustice. Have you started to address how your work situates itself in the context of these emerging questions that this last year has foregrounded for the profession at large?

Adam Fure: I appreciate that question, and I think it's one we need to all ask ourselves and Ellie and I might answer it in different ways. I'm going to try to tie together the Enlightenment comment with this question. Karen Barad wrote a book called *Meeting the Universe Halfway*. She has a doctorate in quantum physics and she's a feminist scholar who teaches at the University of California, Santa Cruz. In this book, she talks about the idea of the light

particle duality and then uses it as a way to describe the world. She says that reality is constantly being produced by both discursive and non-discursive entities that come together to produce reality in real time. For her, a concept doesn't necessarily have a stable meaning as it enters into whatever context shows up, but rather you produce the meaning of a concept in real time, based on how it interacts with other human or non-human entities. That ties into your question because my answer would be a little bit different for each context we work within. We were approached a year and a half ago by a developer who wanted to do affordable housing but wanted to do it inexpensively. It became a game of figuring out what building technologies would get us low enough construction costs so that we could offer rental units at roughly 80% of the median income rate so that more people could afford to rent them. This type of thinking is currently not happening in

Detroit. The current construction costs in the city are a reflection of the only developments that are happening in the city right now, which are almost entirely luxury rental apartments. That project is about providing something that the city needs by rethinking standard construction methods. The client is also engaging community members in the neighborhoods that they're building in to get feedback, so our role is to be a part of that conversation. It's our responsibility to make sure that we're maintaining those project goals, operating in the right way and the best way for the client and community.

Mark Foster Gage: The Karen Barad reference reminds me of something Graham Harman often says about the relationship between global politics and the scientific understanding of the atom. Before the 1940s nobody would have seen much of a relationship between global politics and the physics of the atom, until the nuclear bomb was invented. It linked the splitting of the atom to politics and became one of the most important and defining relationships of the 20th century, via nuclear weapons, the Cold War, and deterrents. These things, which seemed totally separate and unrelated, are in fact deeply united given the right context. The way you talk about studying materials and construction methods as having a potential social impact is interesting because you wouldn't say, "Yes, I'm going to be a socially thoughtful architect. I'm going to really look at materials." One wouldn't make that leap unless you put it in the context of affordability. This is also addressed when you talk about using things within the local area to bring down your costs. There's a lot of things in architecture that we think aren't related yet given closer inspection we find that they are. These relationships are largely undiscovered, particularly with regards

Discussion with
Ellie Abrons and **Adam Fure**

to questions of environmental and social justice. I worry that architecture's current understanding of social engagement is only seen as existing through working for a disadvantaged client. I don't believe that the only way to be doing socially engaged work is by building a cultural center in Africa or building a low-income house. A great alternative example is your material studies that have the potential to lower housing costs by 20%. At face value, material studies come across as having little social engagement, but in this context, they actually play a significant factor.

Ellie Abrons: In some ways the unfortunate thing about architecture is that we have so far to go that almost anything is a step in the right direction. There has been an overwhelming amount of social reckoning recently, in a necessary way that I welcome. It's been a moment of reflection in so many ways. We are also a small business run by four full-time professors, so it's also important to think about how we act ethically in the world according to our values as a small business. This is in addition to thinking about the nature of architectural education in a broad sense as well as just being citizens of the world. Reconsidering how and what we are taught has been one of the primary sites for asking these kinds of questions.

Mark Foster Gage: As educators, we are recalibrated to become educated in some ways.

Vicky Achnani: What is the logic that governs the order of materials and how you put them together in different ways?

Adam Fure: That logic changes. In the Detroit Assembly Plant Project, we made piles of rubble, which was for a speculative project about a particular site in Detroit. For a more recent project, there was also a pile of rubble, but it meant something completely different. Other times it's just a way to save materials that we could then reuse to keep costs down. We navigate each project differently and look for those opportunities where material can come together in ways that are not conventional.

Mark Foster Gage: Given that your rubble piles aren't functioning structurally and aren't functioning programmatically, are you using rubble ornamentally?

Ellie Abrons: We gave a talk at Columbia University several years ago and Ada Tolla, from the firm LOT-EK, was a respondent. She offered a critique along similar lines regarding the project that we did for the Chicago Biennial called "Ghost Box," where we also have piles of rubble. In "Ghost Box," they are ornamental or decorative. In the Detroit Reassembly Plant, even though they're not structural, they are highly spatial and really organize the cinematography of the way in which you would move through that site. They offer a way of seeing things collapsing into images and expanding into three-dimensional spaces.

immediately fall into a category, and you're not sure where it goes, it's probably a good sign that you're doing something right in terms of innovation.

Adam Fure: We're interested in tossing out or at least challenging old binaries, and that includes ornament versus structure. Your work on aesthetics covers this extensively. It's a lazy critique to claim ornament as that which sits on top of something more real. We're interested in material showing up in a purely aesthetic and spatial register and trying to get that to cascade through a series of other reflections or moments that produce a multiplicitous experience. In this experience, some of it feels more visual and some of it feels more tactile. I would be interested in trying to redraw the boundaries of sensible experience in such a way that would problematize this reading of ornament as this extra, decorative, superfluous layer, because that's not how we experience the world.

Mark Foster Gage: When people call my work ornamental it makes me shiver. I hate it. I have no interest in ornament whatsoever. In this new world where we're all testing out new things. It has to be okay to bring outside ideas into the field before you're sure of how it will land in discourse or practice. It's entirely fine if something you're experimenting with is not clearly structural, or not clearly spatial. It's part of the experimentation. In fact, if something lands in architecture that doesn't

Mark Foster Gage: This outdated split goes back to your example from Hal Foster, where James Turrell's work is obscuring all of the truth, and Dan Flavin's work is revealing it. It's untrue when you consider Flavin isn't showing the wires inside the fluorescent tube, or inside the ballast box. There's actually a lot of obscuring there as well. Hal Foster is undeniably hugely influential, however, he is nearly always on the wrong side of things.

Discussion with
Ellie Abrons and **Adam Fure**

Yuyi Shen: The incorporation of emerging technology like photogrammetry clearly plays a role in your work. Is technology something that you are interested in exploring? Do you have an interest in proprietary software, or creating your own definitions that further unravel this correlation between physical and digital?

Ellie Abrons: I'll speak for myself on this and not necessarily for T+E+A+M. Personally, my interest in technology isn't really one that lies in advanced techniques of form-making or fabrication, but rather one about the relationship between the way technology shapes culture at large and the relationship of architecture to that culture. I think a lot about the relationship between the unseen or invisible ways that technology is shaping our lives. How does technology change what it means to be alive? How do we relate to one another as human beings who use technology in almost every aspect of the way in which we interface with the world around us? How can architecture engage with these relationships and play an urgent and critical role in what we should be doing right now? One interesting example is how people don't really say "digital photography" anymore, because there's almost no photography that's not digital photography anymore. In our work, we understand that everything we experience today is being filtered and mediated to a certain degree. This shapes the way we think about putting materials in space but

also putting images in space. We are not big technology people to the extent that we use a lot of sophisticated technology in our design work. When we use photogrammetry, we use the free app you can download on your phone rather than any high-end system. I think we are more down and dirty, more scrappy in the way that we produce our design work with the tools that we have.

Adam Fure: There's a certain expediency to it and that's also part of a post-digital framework. There's still super high-end technological stuff that happens with coding, but there was a time where if an architect wanted to get into coding, they would just learn a coding language and operate at the level of a software engineer. Now software engineers are doing that so expertly that architects don't even get close unless you dedicate many years to developing that expertise. Now there's this larger middle zone where everyone can play around with the vast array of software and apps if they have a smartphone. With regards to whether or not we're interested in making software, I don't think we are. I think this goes back to the question about how we position our work that we do in relation to others. I think there are people that are more directly invested in software, but we like going back and forth between software, apps, and materials. A good example is a project we did for an outdoor pavilion near Chicago in 2017, called

"Living Picture." For the project, we created a 3D Blender model where we painted renderings of the site onto simple shapes and then we had to build them for the competition. To do this we had to recreate the texture maps as full-scale imagery at 100 DPI per one real square inch of printed material. We had to reconstruct the renderings through this elaborate Photoshop process. All the digital artifacts that existed to produce that art stayed around as .png files, and they show up in other places and become part of the work that we do in terms of discursive work. New ways of recombining, reusing, and pulling in different fragments of digital material "stuff" into the constant flow of our own production is what we're interested in.

Ellie Abrons: We design a new workflow for every project we work on. I think that kind of appetite for rethinking the workflow helps us take on different design problems and different projects; it also helps open us up to new trajectories.

Mark Foster Gage: That's important. One of the things I've written about recently is that the architectural community is essentially locked into a standard workflow where you're pushing around boxes in BIM, dragging and dropping insured curtain wall products with a couple options, and dragging and dropping material choices also with a couple choices. That prescribed process of design is producing 99% of the work architects are building, and

Discussion with
Ellie Abrons and **Adam Fure**

most architects use the same software and the same catalogs of the same products. It's like putting a chef at a Taco Bell prep station and saying, "be super creative." When given only a couple inferior ingredients to work with, what is that chef supposed to accomplish? Architects today are the chefs who are just recombining those ingredients into chalupas and gorditos, which get mistaken for creativity. It's just re-assembly. Designing your workflow, as you mention, is one way to free yourself from that deadly process. It's not necessarily the most profitable way out, but it is a way out. I would also agree with your assessment of the architect who designs their own software and are so proud of the software as opposed to what it produces. Now I think there's less of a fetishization of architects doing scripting themselves, and thankfully less of this idea of developing some genius script that only one person has access to. That's so anti-collaborative and anti-discursive. This idea of the solo architectural genius is behind us, and the very structure of T+E+A+M as a collaborative process moves beyond that solo genius model, beyond the idea of some jerk who puts his name on the door and names his practice after himself. We all hate that. That's self-effacing humor for those not paying attention. In any case, can you talk about the role of mentors and peers in the development and success of your work, outside of the members of T+E+A+M?

Adam Fure: We keep talking about that Columbia lecture, so it was evidently important to us. Amale Andraos, the Dean, in that introduction likened us more to a band. I guess a band coming together to produce an album seems like a good analogy for how we work.

Mark Foster Gage: I also spoke with Kristy Balliet and Jimenez Lai a bit about the Possible Mediums conference (or was that a concert?) and its importance to them. You were also part of it. Was that event as important for you as it seemed to be for the two of them?

Adam Fure: Possible Mediums was a project that I put together with Kristy Balliet and two other colleagues that were teaching at different schools. We were all in the Midwest around 2011 or 2012. That original event was so special because, through sixteen or seventeen two-hour workshops, everybody was just working collaboratively with students in the open and it felt significant to all of us because there were no trade secrets. It goes back to your point about the idea of the hidden scripts. Possible Mediums provided a forum to do things and talk about them in real time. That ethos of sharing techniques and sharing ideas was important, and there was this collaborative spirit at the heart of it. At a smaller scale, this was also happening at the University of Michigan with our colleagues. It was partly the reading group on Emilio Ambasz, but we also found our interests starting to merge because we were influencing one another. It made sense to team up and see what would come of us working together. We were young architects, trying to foreground collaboration and work out in the open, and finding different groups of people felt like a very productive space. It was this mutually supportive system as opposed to a competitive or threatening atmosphere. I think that provided an ethos that influenced the move for us four to team up as T+E+A+M.

Ellie Abrons: Being in Ann Arbor has been influential to our understanding of a peer network as well. As I mentioned there's a fellowship program at the University of Michigan that provided the means for many of our peers and colleagues to teach at the school. As Adam mentioned, when Mónica Ponce de León was the dean here she fostered a culture of design and collaboration and brought in a lot of faculty that we consider to be an important part of our peer network.

Mark Foster Gage: Mónica was the dean at the University of Michigan, and when you were still in Michigan she went on to become the dean at Princeton University and subsequently became one of the chairs of the Venice Biennale alongside Cynthia Davidson, where they selected you to participate. There seems to be a strong sense of mentorship there. I believe that, as students or as young teachers, everyone is perfectly capable of equally contributing original ideas to architectural discourse, and you were clearly doing that at the University of Michigan when Mónica was dean there. Clearly, she remembered you several years later and wanted you to represent the United States with those very same ideas that you had started cultivating at Michigan. I'm always fascinated by the role of mentorship in practice, as it's something that's never discussed but is so incredibly important to the development of most practices and positions within discourse. Numerous times I've had a mentorship bolt of lightning that broke open a whole new chapter in my beliefs and practice. I wish those on everybody. It happens through peers as well.

Adam Fure: One thing about the Possible Mediums participants; the four of us were all teaching at different schools, but we were mostly UCLA grads and there were a number of other UCLA grads that were part of the larger group of participants. So many of us had known each other at UCLA and went to school together. Six years later, we were all working in a new capacity as young academics, so we came together to produce this conference, series of events, and eventually a book.

Steven Sculco: You talked a little bit about your experience as teachers and I'm curious about what kinds of design problems you give your students and how that influences your work.

Ellie Abrons: I'll go first and then Adam can go because we actually teach very different things. Over the years I've taught everything from pre-architecture classes for sophomores up to coordinating thesis for the most advanced students. However, for the past couple of years, I've taught a seminar called "Becoming Digital." It's a topical seminar that involves not just architecture students but students from other disciplines as well to study the way that technology has changed the built environment. That has provided an exciting opportunity to connect what we're doing in practice with my teaching. There's often an artificial boundary between the realm of ideas and the realm of practice and I think the more we can connect those things the more excited I am.

Adam Fure: I've been focusing more on introductory studios for both undergraduates

and graduate students, and for the past five or six years I've been a coordinator for the first year of studies. I'm interested in how to break down and introduce the discipline to a group of both new students and students that are more accomplished. I get excited about the problem of describing the discipline through foundational terms.

Samar Halloum: How do you plan for a practice, or do you just allow life to influence you year by year?

Ellie Abrons: We ask ourselves these questions all the time. What are we? What are we investing in, not financially but in terms of what we see for the future. What do we hope for as the impact and scope of our work? Speaking honestly, I think that earlier in your career you are more or less responding to the things in front of you and you're trying to say yes to as many things as possible. We have years of experience now and we are at the cusp of being a building practice, so we want to take advantage of the opportunity to more consciously choose what we do. We want to make sure what we're working on aligns with our values and what we want to put into the world.

Adam Fure: For the client-based work you have to wait and see what comes up. We'll see what we can do when we build something and showing that work to other people will hopefully lead to other opportunities.

Sixth Chapter

Strange Architecture vs. Estrangement

Discussion with
Michael Young
of Young & Ayata

*images versus drawings, questioning
representation, near-future realities, myth
making, qualities of newness*

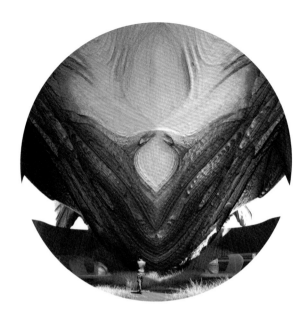

Mark Foster Gage: There are multiple forms of architectural practice, and for the sake of our discussion we will be discussing two; a form of practice invested in solving client's problems versus a form of practice focused on architectural discourse. While investing in solutions for client's problems is not meant to be a criticism because nobody can disagree that the problems need to be solved, architecture also has a two-millennia history of architectural discourse. This is a unique aspect of architecture that not all creative disciplines have. Art and architecture have respective and overlapping discourse, but there is far less of a history of critical discussion in other disciplines like product design, industrial design, fashion, or gastronomy. One thing I love about architecture, something that more lucrative professions can't offer, is the ability to take part in this dialogue with other industries. Architectural discourse folds the invention of new technologies and emerging philosophies into a conversation between architects and the general global marketplace of ideas that define any particular generation. Yes, there are problem-solving practices, however, there are also discourse-based practices that solve the problems clients face while operating with a larger agenda that addresses how architecture fits into the world through various ontological registers. For this series of discussions, I'm interviewing the latter;

architects who are solving problems for clients, being responsible and sustainable, and taking on the responsibility to be active in architectural discourse. Young & Ayata, the practice you share with Kutan Ayata, has been among the most engaged in discourse in recent years. Considering the constantly evolving nature of discourse, can you talk about where you are now with life, practice, and discourse here at the tail end of the COVID pandemic?

Michael Young: I was gone for a year, I mean we've all been gone for a year now because of COVID, but I was in Rome for a year. I was fortunate enough to be there as a fellow of the American Academy. During that time, I was able to reflect on some of the things that we've been doing and thinking about in our office, as well as writing a book. Our practice, Young & Ayata, primarily considers architecture to lie within the realm of a speculative medium. As architects, we speculate on near future realities regarding how we believe the world should look. If we can challenge the assumptions people have about what the world should look like, if we can shift the way that it appears, and if we can alter its presence within our lives— alter attention, shift attention—we begin to open up the world for other possibilities of inhabitation. We do this primarily through aesthetics.

Mark Foster Gage: I've been working on aesthetics as a topic of my writing for quite a while, lately becoming increasingly interested in the work of Boris Groys and his ideas about how we define "newness" as an aesthetic quality. As you discuss architecture as the speculation on a near-newness, with regards to what the world should look like, I wonder how you might tie that together in your work.

Michael Young: We can talk a lot about Boris Groys. Groys has been crucial to my thinking, particularly his books *On the New* and *In the Flow*, which have been both important to me and our practice. For architects, a building is a mediation, a text is a mediation, and images are a mediation. We are immersed in these worlds, so we have to take them seriously. We have to take their aesthetics seriously. Aesthetics in the senses is not just about beauty. It's not just about categorizing the ways in which people argued aesthetics through the 18th and 19th century, where one becomes attuned as an elite aesthete of the world. None of that is what we're talking about when we talk about aesthetics. We are talking about something much more primal in terms of the ways in which we understand reality to appear. When I use the word realism, it's not about a naive realism, or a pictorial naturalism or something along those lines. Architects redistribute our assumptions about the way in which reality appears. We can talk about

Nation reports, more global citizens live in cities rather than rural areas. This massive switch from rural to urban that has taken place in our lifetimes is rather incredible. When the majority of people open their front door their world is defined by buildings in cities, rather than rural landscapes. Architecture is now responsible, in the way it hasn't quite been in the past, for producing the backdrop of reality.

Michael Young: If we're talking about Boris Groys, we might as well delve further into it. It's important to our practice and I believe contemporary architectural discourse in general. My thirteen-year-old and eight-year-old children are really into the Disney+ TV show *The Mandalorian.* I was listening to an interview in which Jon Favreau, the creator of the show, was explaining how it's important when you're making a film to take a mundane thing and elevate its importance, so that people begin to watch the movie differently. At the same time, you can take really special things that people love and dirty them up and grind them up. This left me thinking, "Oh man, Jon Favreau is reading Boris Groys," because that's a significant aspect of his writing. This reminds me of something that happened not long ago regarding our work on the site DADA Daily. A former employee of ours, Mor Segal, sent us a link to this site. The reason she sent it to us was not because of what DADA Daily was selling, things like a candle where the

it in Boris Groys's terms as a cultural exchange, where the profane and the sacred are shifting places.

Mark Foster Gage: Not surprisingly I agree with you. Architecture is about more than solving individual problems as proposed by clients, it's the discipline that is now most responsible for defining what reality looks like for humankind. As recent as the last ten years, according to United

Discussion with
Michael Young

Sixth Chapter
Strange Architecture vs. Estrangement

127

middle finger is the only part of the hand that doesn't melt. It's kind of funny, you light the hand, you put it on your table and it's pretty weird. The reason she sent this post to us was because of the still life painting in the background. The people were selling the hand candle against a still life background that was specifically of interest to us because we made it. Young & Ayata made that background image as part of a conceptual project in our office. We'll get to that in a second. On the still life image, there's a vase that we designed, a rendering of an object that we made, and on that object is a drawing that we had done years before. Eventually, we physically made these vases to test the limits of texture, color, ornament, and decoration through 3D printing. We wanted to see if we could get associations to come

Discussion with
Michael Young

through the 3D printer that were in excess of the powder that was being printed. For us, it was a question of realism. It was a question of disturbing the reality of what we were looking at and what we were making and consider how a new reality was understood. For architects, the way in which one ornaments an object like this vase can shift its materiality. We can cause it to allude other associations allied with other materials, or other effects, or other kinds of properties. Through all of this, the designer, in this case, us, has changed the reality of the object one thought one was looking at. To test this even further, we started photo-realistically collaging the vases into seventeenth-century Dutch still life paintings.

Mark Foster Gage: Why did you choose the Dutch still life as a backdrop to place your work?

Michael Young: The Dutch still life, or rather the genre of the still life in general, is kind of an amazing thing. It is a genre of painting that has been historically diminished as something not as important as paintings with more dramatic narratives. Still life paintings are about the ways in which one can represent the world realistically, but in fact, they're incredibly artificial. They use all of the techniques of the painter to begin to build a believable world, but the believable world is not

really a world that is inhabited. It's a world of perfect reflections, colors, textures, luminosity, and viscosity. So, we photo-realistically collaged our vase into a historic Dutch still life painting, and then we sent it to some people and asked them what they thought. We knew it was working because people came back to us and said, "Yeah that's a nice still life, but I don't understand it. What did you do?" At some level, the realism of the rendering had entered a level of believability that it could become part of that still life configuration.

Mark Foster Gage: So, DADA Daily had used a historic Dutch still life that,

unbeknownst to them, included your 21st-century vase rendering itself with an older 21st-century drawing on it?

Michael Young: Exactly. I contacted them, and I said, "Hey, that's great. Thanks for doing that." They responded, "What are you talking about?" They didn't even realize that they were taking our image, which we had taken from another person. For us, that was great. It actually made the point better than we could have made ourselves. The fact that they jacked something into an image that we had jacked into, perpetuates over hundreds of years a constant question about the ways in which one can image

Discussion with
Michael Young

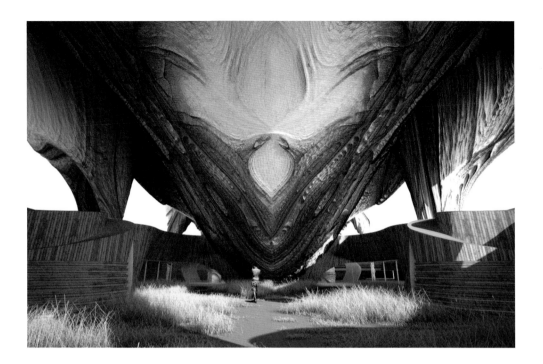

the world. This is also part of the ways in which I think we see practice today, in the necessity to take the image seriously.

Mark Foster Gage: Would it be accurate to describe your practice as having a larger interest in addressing architectural representation in a new way?

Michael Young: I've taught representation courses for years, and it absolutely impacts our work. The discipline itself has the tendency to privilege the aesthetic effects of drawing and to devalue the aesthetic effects of images. By this I mean that architectural drawings are disciplinary; they have disciplinary value historically within architecture through their rigor, geometry, construction, and their abstraction. Images are devalued as extra disciplinary, or non-architectural, because they are thought to be for the consumption and seduction of those who are non-architects. This is a problem in a number of ways. Firstly, everything we produce through a computer is an image. We can render our digital models to look like drawings if we want to, but we have to understand what a drawing looks like as an image in order to render it to look like a drawing. When the only reason for making an image look like a drawing is because drawings are part of architecture's historical discourse,

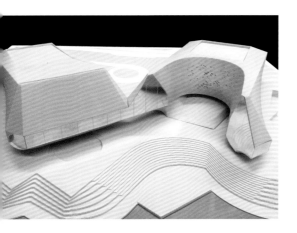

this practice should be questioned. It's important for architecture to address images today in addition to this previously exclusive interest in drawings. We are immersed in a world of images now. We build our world out of images that are constantly being montaged and re-manipulated. Over and over again, we send images into our phones and onto our screens where they are subsequently devoured and consumed by us—and consequently, they are telling us the way the world should look. Today we need to take images very seriously as architects.

Mark Foster Gage: There seems to be a divide in the profession between photo-realistic images that are produced via rendering, and collage. The more conservative side of architecture says that such images are only used by corporate offices to sell projects. The attitude here is that only through our secret architectural language

of drawings can we understand the true nature of the building. Renderings are seen as a veneer over some unseen truth, which is a distant vestige of the Frankfurt School and the historical popularity of the Critical Theory in architecture, which came to be known more specifically as the "Critical Project" in architecture just prior to the turn of the millennium. I also believe that today, given the amount of images we consume and the power they have over us, architects desperately need to develop intelligence with images in the same way we have for drawings since the early Renaissance. If we stick with drawings and ignore images, we're bringing a knife to a gun fight. I think images are where we can be more speculative, but in a more democratic language that you don't need to be a trained architect to understand. I love a good architectural drawing as much as the next architect, but I think architecture's near future, in terms of both discourse and practice, is through images and their ability to realistically speculate about future realities.

Michael Young: The book that I recently finished is called *Reality Modeled After Images*. This book traces a history of imaging and its role in architectural representation. It takes the stance that imaging in architecture has actually been theoretically addressed and is a fundamental part of our discipline, perhaps only recently forgotten in favor of drawings. Images have gone through multiple transformations within architecture over the last several centuries. The book is structured around three words from the École des Beaux-Arts. These three terms were commonplace at the École des Beaux-Arts to describe every drawing that was rendered for disciplinary discourse and debate. These were: poché, entourage, and mosaïque. Specifically, poché is a rendering technique, the graphic infill, the tone, the wash, or the hatch used to articulate walls that have been cut through. Entourage refers to all that is not architecture, the landscape, the trees, etc. Eventually, in the 20th century, entourage became things like people, furniture, artwork, and other objects like cars. Mosaïque is the articulation of the surface

rendered into the drawing, the ornament and the decoration, the patterning.

Mark Foster Gage: Your claim is that poché, entourage, and mosaïque have some relationship to architectural representation that goes beyond drawing?

Michael Young: These three words were as theoretical as much as they were words about imaging. They not only allowed the visualizations of an idea to become legible to an audience that understood how to read them, but they also brought the idea into a realm of strange realism. This means that the production of the École des Beaux-Arts was using techniques to render things close to reality while maintaining a disciplinary distance. This can be observed in the pink-washing of poché, treating the

thickness as a kind of space between the inside and the outside. The coloration represents a space no longer real but somehow hyper-real, floating between realities, floating between the entourage and the mosaïque. This distancing can also be seen in the shadow of a section cut, where shading is rendered in a way that could never actually exist. In reality, the building is not being cut in half. There's no sunlight that comes straight through the section cut of the project, but it's represented realistically as such. This is within the realm of strange realism. Furthermore, these three concepts within the École des Beaux-Arts are alive and well today, not only in architecture but also for the purposes of imaging the world using LiDAR, Photogrammetry, Neural Networks, AI analysis, photo analysis, facial recognition software, etc. These are the technologies through which our attention is constantly monitored, in the images that we are consuming, online, digitally, through the internet.

Mark Foster Gage: How did you become an architect who is interested in this particular discourse? You seem to have picked up numerous interests in your architectural career, ranging from the École des Beaux-Arts, to the subject of representation, to an interest in advanced technologies. One of the things I'd like to tease out in these interviews is the idea that, as architects moving through the world, we each pick up different little Easter eggs along the

way and these become significant ideas on how we practice and contribute to architectural discourse. I'm interested in the influences that led to these moments and how they affect the development of each respective architect. As you went through life, into school, through the professional world, and into your own practice, how did you pick up these interests? What was the role of mentorship during that trajectory?

Michael Young: When you look back and try to figure these things out, you realize that there are certain threads that are always there. You may think, "Oh my God, I'm going through so many changes," but then you realize you've essentially been doing the same thing over and over again. I think you and I share the fact that our undergraduate education and entry into the profession was pre-computer, pre-digital in a way. Computers existed in the early '90s, but they weren't used in architecture nearly as much as they were even a decade later. You and I started architecture school in the early '90s, so we were taught to draw using more traditional methods: descriptive geometry, ink on mylar paper, ways of building up shade and shadow and tone through ink washes and watercolors. However, by the time you and I had entered graduate school, the field had become nearly fully digitized. Most students by 2000 were doing the majority of their projects on the computer as opposed to hand drawing, as they would have been in 1990.

Discussion with
Michael Young

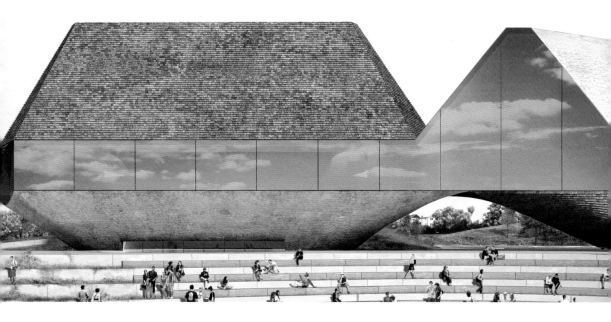

I was in graduate school in the early 2000s at Princeton and I believe you were at Yale roughly the same time. I remember when Rhino was released, and all the students received free copies. I got it, opened it up, and I thought, "Well I guess we're going to learn this now." While we learned and used these programs—and perhaps we weren't yet aware of this—they were really asking us to think differently about representation and therefore how we visualized and imaged the world.

Mark Foster Gage: This is true, our generation probably witnessed the most dramatic and immediate shift in architectural representational techniques ever in the history of humanity. While perspective was re-discovered by Brunelleschi in the early 15th century, it took a century for its use and understanding to become widespread in the discipline of architecture. That century-long change became a decade-long change for us, meaning that it could be witnessed in a single lifetime, unlike the influence of perspective. We'll likely be the last generation to be able to complain about how we used to use pencils and walked to school uphill both ways…

Michael Young: One of the phrases I've started to use to address these ideas is "conventions of representation." I think the importance in knowing the conventions

of representation lies in our ability to subsequently dismantle them. A lot of those conventions have been used to defend the discipline from change, and when digital technology started coming in, they forced us to look at our systems of operating and representing architecture.

Mark Foster Gage: Has this shift impacted your practice?

Michael Young: It wasn't a belief in our office that somehow digital technologies were the solution to anything in particular, as if they should be lauded and applauded and used as an expression of an architecture that was contemporary. It was necessary to use these tools because they were clearly changing how everything in architecture operated. We wanted to figure out how they're changing things, why, and what the fallout for the discipline would be. So, we tried to figure out what from the pre-digital should stay, what should go, and what we needed to do differently.

Mark Foster Gage: Architects don't develop alone in a vacuum. I've found time and again that a particularly important indicator of what your discursive interests will be is directly related to whom you come in contact with throughout your education. Not that you necessarily follow their interests, but you are forced to reckon with their ideas and develop yours in relation to them. The luckiest of us have architectural mentors that encourage us to do this. Did

you have such mentors or influential figures in your development as a student and architect?

Michael Young: An early and influential mentorship developed for me when I started working as Peter Eisenman's teaching assistant at Yale in 2005, which I think is when I met you. At the time I was interested in the manner in which architectural representation had changed over time, and how this could become a theoretical issue to be explored by contemporary architecture. The discourse started much more

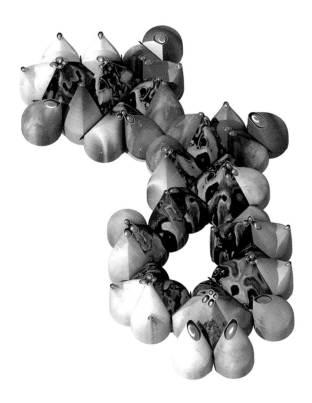

along those lines than, say, the digital as an aesthetic that should be expressed in digital work. Because we had to teach in the context of the digital, Peter and I had to learn what was going on with it and theorize an agenda around it which was largely about representation.

Mark Foster Gage: I think people who enter the world of architectural discourse in their practice first need some sort of Charon-like figures who ferry us into it. I don't think students naturally default to deep discussions about contemporary

architectural history. It seems that most architectural theory courses are in fact histories of architectural theory. I'm always surprised how little students are introduced to the discussions happening today. However, once a group of students is introduced, it seems like a little fire is lit and peer-groups develop that continue to address certain issues. I wonder how the role of your peers was influential to your development. I'm asking the architects in these discussions this question in particular as I think students should be on the lookout for

significant moments in their own architectural trajectory. What do those moments look like, and how do people their own age nourish their beliefs?

Michael Young: One of the things that Peter Eisenman taught me was that there were problems within architecture that have a historical dimension. If you can tap into this it means you are able to bring a historical relation to the discipline into a contemporary situation.

Mark Foster Gage: I think that's an important point, that part of architectural discourse is also having dialogues with architects that may have been dead for centuries or even millennia. Some conversations take place over centuries, and they require a significant historical knowledge about the field. I will say, this has always been one of the more enjoyable aspects of a discourse-based practice. I see my work as a way of creating a dialogue with the work of past architects, such as, Plečnik, William Burges, and a host of others who are rarely, if ever, covered in architectural schools.

Michael Young: For me, that was Borromini and baroque architecture; I had always been interested in them. It wasn't until Peter Eisenman helped me to discursively access that, where it all of a sudden became a contemporary problem for me to deal with. Regarding other mentors, Jesse Reiser and Nanako Umemoto (RUR) were crucial for both Kutan Ayata and myself. Kutan worked for them for four years, I worked for them briefly.

Discussion with
Michael Young

Mark Foster Gage: And you had Jesse Reiser as a professor.

Michael Young: I had Jesse Reiser as a professor at Princeton University. Also, Edward Eigen, who teaches at Harvard Graduate School of Design, taught me at Princeton. He is one of the smartest and most interesting architectural thinkers I know, in terms of knowledge about the history of science and the history of technology. He introduced me to the work of Bruno Latour, all of the connections that go back through the history of science come from him. Through the work of Bruno Latour, I got into a dialogue with the work of the philosopher Graham Harman, who David Ruy also knew. So these things all begin to link together. The other mentor I'll mention is Miles Ritter, who you've likely never

heard of. Miles Ritter taught me descriptive geometry and projective geometry at Princeton. He has never written, he's never published, but has extensive knowledge on architectural representation in terms of its histories, and its links to computation and digital technologies. He knows more about that stuff than anyone I've ever come across. Anyway, I just wanted to acknowledge the influences he's had on me and, in a way, encourage you to find those kinds of people. They're out there and they're amazing.

Mark Foster Gage: That's my experience as well, that all faculty and people don't impact you equally. It's massively lopsided. I think there have probably been five people in my life who determined my entire architectural direction. What role have your peers played in your continued development as an architect and architectural thinker?

Michael Young: Peers are incredibly important. Nobody does anything by themselves, and nobody does anything of value alone. In my case, I have a partnership with Kutan Ayata, but I think there's a fundamental necessity for you to also find a larger group of people that you don't necessarily agree with all the time, but who you share a set of interests with. Peers with whom you talk, argue, and share your work and ideas with. You and I have been talking to each other for the last fifteen years and there's a whole group of people roughly our age we discuss things with as well. It's important for architects to find people within their own generation—however one defines that generation—that you feel that you belong to, and it's important to not necessarily agree with them. Disagreement allows discussion and discourse to happen, it's a tool for trying to understand what activates and motivates you, personally, as an architect. That in itself is a crucial thing for you to identify.

Mark Foster Gage: Are there some people in contemporary discourse that you disagree with in a dramatic way, and why? Or the reverse, is there a cabal you run with?

Michael Young: There is a kind of Venn diagram that crosses over through different things. As far as the architects within my loosely defined "generation," there's a group that I am in dialogue with, which includes David Ruy, Karel Klein, Ferda Kolatan, Rhett Russo, Jason Payne, and you. We've been talking for the past decade about a handful of issues that cross through philosophy and aesthetics. I was also part of a conference and workshop called Possible Mediums. That was the first time I met Andrew Holder, Adam Fure, Ellie Abrons, and Kristy Balliet, who I am also in dialogue with. I consider myself in between generations because when I went to graduate school, I had already worked for an architect in San Francisco for six years. So in graduate school I was with a group of people who were slightly younger than me, but my friends were the people who are slightly older than me. People like Jimenez Lai and Andrew Atwood are good friends of mine now, but they're in the generation of slightly younger architects. There's this interesting pressure from younger architects that are doing work that you don't quite fully understand, but you know has something really good in it. That feeling forces me to try to further understand my own motivations, to try and change in order to at least address the new things that are being identified. Another person who's been a good friend for years is Liam Young. I agree with Liam about the use of multiple mediums as speculations, especially in cinematography and the ways in which scenarios in near future situations can play out. As an architect we're always

designing for the near future. We're never designing the present. We're always thinking about that which can be slightly other than we assume it to be. I think Liam's work is great, with respect to that. The disagreement I have with Liam is that I also think it's important to build. Liam doesn't think it's important to build at all, so at that point, we disagree.

Mark Foster Gage: And who do you disagree with in your discursive position?

Michael Young: The people that I find that I disagree with a lot tend to all have some relationship with OMA or Rem Koolhaas. It's interesting because OMA is one of my favorite architecture firms, ever. I think their work is incredible, but they've produced a kind of lineage of architects whose work I'm not as interested in. I find the work of these architects' problematic for discourse and pedagogy. Some of those architects are very talented and do very good

work and can do great things. However, there's a dependence and/or desire for the blunt level, total clarity of the diagram as the alibi to communicate, and to explain everything that is within the architectural proposition. Those are usually the architects I find myself arguing with.

Mark Foster Gage: I agree that these architects are very talented in a lot of ways, but I regret for many of them that they are not in dialogue with any architectural history or any discourse. Which is what is lost when you believe that something as complex as a piece of architecture, a building, can be existentially distilled into a diagram with a bunch of arrows on it; Every project is self-contained to its own problems, and I think that's very problematic if we want to collectively produce the aforementioned backdrop of reality in the world today. Architecture needs to be more than solving individual problems in a self-contained

project. The easy architecture that gives you instant answers is the opposite of discourse; it's the immediate and satisfying, not the questioning deep dive—something that you and I enjoy—that makes the architectural profession unique.

Michael Young: My brother is an architect as well and he has a practice in Brooklyn. So, having two sons who do this, my mother has been interested in figuring out whatever this architecture thing actually is. She calls me up one day, and she says, "You know I just watched this TED Talk with this Bjarke Ingels architect, do you know who that is?" "Yeah Mom," I tell her, "I know who that is." She then says, "I finally understand what you do. What you do is so cool. What you do is so exciting. I finally get it after all these years of you telling me about what you're trying to do

and me never really understanding you. I now finally understand it. It's because of Bjarke Ingels." There's something funny about that, right? That's pretty powerful. If he's able to get my mom to all of a sudden understand her sons' occupation in terms that she hadn't thought through before, he's doing something right. But I guess the issue is, and I think we probably agree on this Mark, what she now thinks I do is not what I do at all.

Mark Foster Gage: That trajectory of architecture is about providing people with answers, and it often manifests as digestible, simple diagrams. I would say our trajectory of architecture is about inviting users to ask questions. I am more interested in producing a state of fascination or curiosity than doing something so easily and purposefully consumable.

Discussion with
Michael Young

Michael Young: Absolutely.

Samar Halloum: How did you decide to start your office and did that happen while you were teaching? How did you make that decision?

Michael Young: As Mark mentioned, he was a post-professional student, meaning he already had a professional degree in architecture prior to graduate school. I was also a post-professional student. Prior to this, as I mentioned previously, I worked for an architect in San Francisco for six years. This was during the late '90s dot-com boom, and we were building a lot at that time. After six years with that practice, I realized that it wasn't the way I could imagine spending the rest of my life as an architect. So, I went to graduate school for a post-professional degree, specifically because I knew I wanted to get into teaching.

Mark Foster Gage: Once you started teaching, how did start your own practice? What made your practice different from the practice you were with in San Francisco?

Michael Young: People have different opinions about this, but I believe that it's a really good idea to find a partner to start a practice with. I need somebody to talk ideas through, and that's something that Kutan and myself do constantly. It's become integral to our process to hash it out, argue about the work, and develop things off of each other. Our practice started shortly after I started teaching at Cooper Union around 2005. During the summers I was working for other architects such as RUR, Stan Allen, and a few others. I reached a moment, I don't know exactly what it was, where I thought, "I don't need to do this for other people, I can do this myself." I knew everything I needed to know to do it, and Kutan shared those sentiments, so we decided to start an office.

Mark Foster Gage: How do your practice, teaching, and writing interlace with one another?

Michael Young: A lot of the architects we've touched on have developed a symbiosis between their practice and their pedagogy, and this is absolutely the case for us. There are things that we develop in studios and seminars that we then bring into the office, and systems we developed in the office that we try to teach

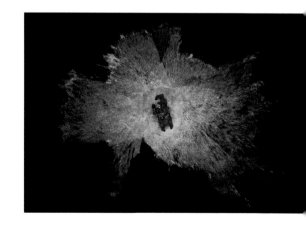

Discussion with
Michael Young

within studios and seminars. At the same time, there's a middle ground where writing and research continuously develop. So, our practice is interested in architectural discourse as much as it is in trying to get a new commission to build. All that said, we absolutely do want to build. We want to build more, and to be honest, we thought we would've probably built more by now.

Mark Foster Gage: Don't we all…

Michael Young: We've been doing this since 2008 and sure, we thought we would have built much more over the last ten years, but we finished a ground-up building last year in Mexico City that we're happy with. It might take a decade to finally get a building that you're happy with, but that's okay. We're on it and we're moving on to the next thing.

Elise Limon: What are the most frustrating things that accompany the way in which you think and theorize about architecture within your practice as you go through the process of seeing a built project through?

Michael Young: The Mexico City project is actually a good example of the relationship between theoretical work and built work. That project can be argued as an estrangement of poché. Two chapters in this book are on poché and there are other arguments I've been making for years about estrangement. That's the way I argue that project to myself and to my students.

When I go down to the client in Mexico City I don't say, "Hire us, we're going to estrange your poché." That sounds insane. What we do say is that by rotating the windows, every single space has a view that's oblique, that looks out to the street or to the site. The neighbors can build up to the lot lines and yet every single bedroom along the edges of the building will constantly have an unobstructed, oblique view to the city beyond, or to the street beyond. It's also a way of giving the occupant consistent daylight, all because these windows rotate into the building.

Mark Foster Gage: There are often aspects of projects that speak more to clients and aspects that speak more to architects and architectural discourse. Charles Jencks called this "double-coding." I've always thought a project's layered "coding" can and should work simultaneously. A chef in a restaurant, for example, is making you dinner that tastes good and will satisfy and nourish you. That chef is also making that same meal to earn money to pay for his own life. Some chefs are also making that meal to develop their own language, perhaps to get some notice in the industry or a Michelin star. So, the same plate of food in a restaurant can have multiple ambitions, which I think is the same with architecture.

Michael Young: The windows on that project do things that are good for the client and their home, but the way they are situated is also an argument about poché,

an argument about windows doing things that windows don't usually do. It is an argument that will change your perception between interior and exterior and allow people to hopefully inhabit these apartments in some unique manner. However, the language does shift when you're speaking to different audiences. I think we all know this, and I think that's actually a good thing to keep in mind. The audience in which you are addressing matters greatly. It doesn't change the content of the concepts, but it changes the articulation of the ways in which one expresses those ideas.

Mark Foster Gage: In the process of conceptualizing and speaking about architecture as a debate between function and concept, there is still plenty of room for aesthetics. For the last century, architects have no history when it comes to

Discussion with
Michael Young

Michael Young: Absolutely.

Vicky Achnani: Something you spoke about earlier was your interest in interrogating "newness." How has that evolved throughout the duration of your practice in terms of technology? How does your process account for external changes that produce new tools or forms of innovation?

Michael Young: When there's change in technology it leads to new forms of mediation. My book tracks that mediation, covering the history of imaging in architecture from the École des Beaux-Arts until today in order to dispel a bit of technological determinism. I don't believe that the computer or the software is what causes the change. Sure, working digitally is different from working by hand, but more importantly, working with the aesthetic values of the image is different from working with the aesthetic values of the drawing. That value difference provokes a more substantial question than whether something is drawn by hand or drawn on a computer, and it's part of the argument of the book. I'm noticing an interesting change when I consider the way we invested in digital tools 15 years ago. Developing a digital modeling skillset meant getting really good at one software. Now my students have this ability to shift between dozens of different software packages and platforms, and it seems effortless. It reminds me a little bit of that *Matrix* scene where Neo gets Kung-Fu downloaded into his brain.

discussing things in aesthetic terms. We have no language to discuss the aesthetics of a project without being punished for being overly concerned about frivolous things like beauty. This is an issue because projects do have aesthetic dimensions and non-architects usually judge buildings solely by these criteria. I think it's a disciplinary deficit that we have to overcome, and one that we don't have a language for.

We might ask someone at the office to use Mudbox to deform a surface and she'll say, "I don't know Mudbox." She'll then come back seconds later and say, "but I can learn it. I'll do it tomorrow." That's amazing to me because my brain doesn't work like that at all. My skillset's relationship to software is actually very slow compared to the ways in which this younger generation is engaging with these things.

Mark Foster Gage: I was educated as a classical architect and the use of poché is naturally second nature to me. I never knew of the alternative until well after graduation. I like to shape rooms, spaces, and volumes and to do this you usually need to use poché. In fact, our coffee shop at Notre Dame was called "Café Poché." I'm a bit of an anachronist, but it was certainly an architectural faux pas to use poché in the 20th century.

Michael Young: Nobody used the word poché for the first fifty years of the 20th century because it was associated with bad, academic, Beaux-Arts architecture. If one was truly to be modern with a free plan, you didn't need poché. In fact, poché was the "paralyzed plan" in Corbusier's language, and so architects wanted to push that away. Robert Venturi brought it back with totally different terms. It was no longer about solidity. You can have a thinness outside and a thinness inside. The friction and difference and tension between those two was like poché, without solid mass.

You can have Frank Gehry doing poché architecture, with radically different thin surfaces on the inside and on the outside, and the inter-mixture in between becomes zones of movement, zones of structure, zones of informal spaces in the pockets of the poché. In our longer discursive journey here, we see Venturi as a discursive disciplinary architect. Like Boris Groys, he was taking terms that had been devalued and was revaluing them within a different situation. At the same time, he was taking valued terms from modernism and labelling them superfluous, sending them into the realm of the profane and shifting discourse into what is retrospectively described as postmodernism.

Taiga Taba: You've discussed the value of parafictional work and how it forces us to ask questions, instead of giving us answers. How do you see this influencing the discourse of architecture and its practices in the future?

Michael Young: Parafiction is a tool for mining reality. It's not a controversial opinion to say that architecture is one of the things that establishes the ways in which people assume reality to look. I walk past architecture every day, and when I walk down the street I don't really notice it. The majority of built work is sent to the background yet it establishes the ways in which I think my world operates, looks, behaves, feels, sounds. It forms that reality. Architects have the chance to disturb that

Discussion with
Michael Young

reality, not by offering an escape through fantasy, but by making one pay attention to it, elongating one's attention to it, making one question the ways in which certain things have become built or constructed or manifested. This so-called background is built, it is constructed, it is artifice. Parafictional art allows us to not only reveal that artifice, but use the revelation of artifice, to propose alternate manners of inhabiting a planet. It unlocks a doubt about the world you are looking at, after you've accepted that reality. To a large extent, this doesn't require any training; you just need senses, eyeballs, and history of existing in the world, to realize the ways in which it's operating.

Mark Foster Gage: That differs from propaganda, which generally has a specific function to change your mind about something, whereas parafiction invites you to be curious about the reality you take for granted. It's a relatively new discourse, ten to fifteen years old at the most, which is exciting. The term doesn't even have a Wikipedia page yet.

Michael Young: All architects and all architecture operate parafictionally to some degree; the building is not there, the life that the building will influence is not there, the material is not there. Our design work is a speculation on the ways in which that reality will be, will behave, will alter, will look, will feel. We should be thinking about architecture in parafictional terms because we are proposing fictions as realities. If we take that proposition seriously—and we should—it's much more profound than simply satisfying certain necessities.

Mark Foster Gage: That's an important point. Our profession has begun to address important questions more openly about justice, equality and socially engaged architecture. However, I worry about the way we assess success using these registers. There is no guarantee that the building is going to be just and operate in a socially conscious way even if an architect has ethical intentions for their building to operate in that way. Social justice through architecture starts as speculation and desire, and these goals can easily remain unrealized. There is no guarantee that righteousness in the soul of the architect translates into righteousness in the performance of the building. As architects we need to be careful about what we claim our architecture to be and what we claim our buildings accomplish. We need to be more humble about the different possible impacts of our work as it inhabits the future. I think humility is actually a big part of being speculative in discourse and practice.

Michael Young: I think that's true. Our world is precarious right now, and so is our involvement with it. A good dose of humility and humbleness is necessary and important.

Seventh Chapter

Post-Digital Play and Other Possible Mediums

Discussion with
Jimenez Lai and **Kristy Balliet**
of Bureau Spectacular and Bair Balliet

utopia as a journalistic tool, collaborations and peer-networks between young architects, institutional innovation, the quality of character, the aesthetics of effort

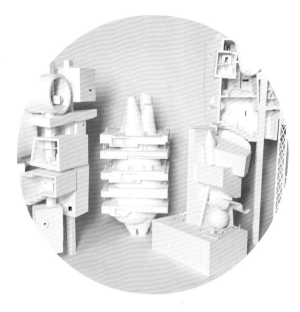

Mark Foster Gage: I wanted to interview you both together as I think you offer two very distinct positions in the larger umbrella movement of what has been labeled, for better or for worse, the "post digital" in architecture. I should note that this idea in architecture is not positioned against the use of digital technologies, but rather focusses on not fetishizing these technologies to the degree that the digital formalism in architecture did, between 2000-2010. A lot is going on in this large umbrella, but I chose you two because Kristy has a very explicit interest in the three-dimensional qualities of volume; projects are puffy and seemingly filled with air. Jimenez, on the other hand, has probably the closest relationship

to two-dimensional practice that one could possibly have as an architect.

Jimenez Lai: There have been two continuous aspects about my work. Firstly, cartoons about architecture, where a cartoon is the medium and architecture is the subject matter. And conversely, there's a different and second stream of my work which I would call "cartoonish architecture," where cartoon is the sensibility and architecture is the medium. So that's the key distinction to draw between these two; Cartoons about architecture, and cartoonish architecture. These ideas also speak to whether or not architecture is something to be built or to be designed, versus

Discussion with
Jimenez Lai and **Kristy Balliet**

architecture as a representation of stories to be told. This is a clear line that I like to draw. If we were to go to the editorial segment of newspapers, the function of cartoons is always political, especially when some type of parody or parable is being told.

Mark Foster Gage: Communication is a historic part of architecture, but one that has largely been forgotten in favor of all the other means of communication we have at our disposal. Can you talk about that role of communication in architecture a bit more, and how it plays out differently in your work than it has historically?

Jimenez Lai: The riverbank of the LA River, once upon a time, was a favorite playground for graffiti artists, so let's think about the function of graffiti. It's not just an expression. Its role is to "tag," and to tag is to declare presence. In the more severe cases, it is a declaration of presence as a gang member. In this latter case, it is a means of declaring of territory, politically. It is a political demarcation of presence. This kind of instinct to declare presence still exists within all of us somehow—from history through today. I can't tell you the number of times I have gone to visit some type of monument and some people have carved a heart that says, "T + J" or something along those lines. This instinct goes as far back as rock art when we look at cave paintings. The LA riverbank is a type of cave painting at the scale of the city. However, being at the scale of the city, the LA riverbank had every single piece of graffiti on it erased when the most powerful gang in Los Angeles swooped down some time in the 1990s. I'm talking, of course, about the city of Los Angeles as that gang. They politically came down and declared that no gangs get to declare presence. It was the city of Los Angeles declaring its presence and that presence is white.

Mark Foster Gage: That's a very Modernist mentality for the city of Los Angeles to have, that pure whiteness is somehow neutral and internationally acceptable by all. What you suggest is that in this case white isn't the absence of a color, it's actually another tag by a group that is declaring its presence, in this case, it is the city of Los Angeles.

Jimenez Lai: Architectural Modernism offered a type of utopian idea, but architectural "utopias" never really follow their own rules. They aren't a future projection of unrealistic things; rather they always seem to be a hyperbolic representation of the societal problems that already exist in any given moment. Take the young Italians of Superstudio from the 1960s, for example. They weren't really proposing a continuous monument of glass and brick and so forth, no, they were talking about their concerns of a society experiencing the end of modernism. Even your own proposal for shutting off the East River in New York City was a utopian project. You were addressing a contemporary societal concern, and I think that's the function of

Discussion with
Jimenez Lai and **Kristy Balliet**

these kinds of journalistic presences. I've been thinking a lot about where we are and where we're going. Kristy and I are in the category of the post-digital for these interviews, but I would like to think that we're something else, we're entering a different stage in contemporary culture. I've been listening a lot to contemporary philosophers who talk about the classification of the "isms" that we're within, and the oscillation between irony and sincerity is one where I would say my generation lies.

Mark Foster Gage: How did the two of you meet and how did your worlds collide? Maybe you can fold that into a broader circle about the *Possible Mediums* workshop and conference in 2013, and how that came about. I may be over emphasizing the importance of that moment but that's when my architectural peers and I started to realize who you were and what your ideas were about.

Kristy Balliet: I think a lot of it had to do with geography and timing, like most things. I think it was right around 2010-2011 when a large group of us had recently been hired in faculty positions in the Midwest. As you know, in the Midwest what is "nearby" sort of expands. I think it was no accident that as a bunch of new faculty members at a series of Midwestern schools were beginning to work on their own research projects in earnest, there was an active search for each of us to find our nearby peers.

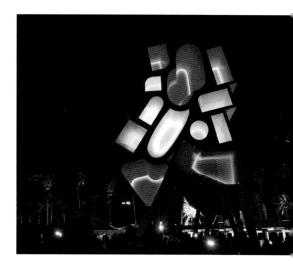

Mark Foster Gage: Being from Nebraska, the nearby comment makes sense to me. My parents didn't want me going far away for school, so I went to the University of Notre Dame for my undergraduate degree. Notre Dame is a nine-hour drive from Omaha, but it wasn't considered "far away." Of course, these distances all collapsed with the emergence of the internet, which didn't really exist for the public when I started college. There's a certain irony here though, being that it was mostly young architects from my generation, my peers of the same age, who were so interested in "the digital," ended up filling a lot of the east and west coast teaching positions. This left the available teaching jobs, for a time, in the Midwest. It actually worked in your favor because it allowed you and your peers to discursively influence an entire region, in a sense.

Seventh Chapter
Post-Digital Play and Other Possible Mediums

155

Kristy Balliet: For sure. I think we're all maybe a bit uneasy with labels at the moment, as things are still developing, but I certainly understand that as a kind of post-digital moment. I think many of us had been invited to these institutions to elevate the digital, to bring in and develop our individual architectural projects and discourses, but to also do a lot of heavy lifting in terms of bringing those institutions into the fold of a larger discourse. We were asked to expand conversations at our

schools, and in order to do that, we reached out to peers at other nearby institutions that were working on similar issues.

Mark Foster Gage: What institutions and people?

Kristy Balliet: I was at Ohio State University at the time, and I was most initially in contact with Kelly Bair, who's now my business partner. At the time we were just Midwestern colleagues, and she was at the University of Illinois in Chicago. Adam Fure was at the University of Michigan and Kyle Miller was at the University of Kentucky. Coincidentally, we were all UCLA graduates between 2003 and 2006, although we did not all know each other when we were in graduate school. I think when we found ourselves in the Midwest, we also found ourselves tasked with developing our own discourse vis-à-vis this common DNA and interests. So, we began to connect with one another and invite each other for reviews and look at each other's work. That quickly expanded to other peers at those institutions, and we started to realize that in order to really have an impact at any one of our individual institutions, we needed to avoid siloed conversation within each of our schools. We needed to, and wanted to, plan a larger event that could impact all of our schools. That is how the Possible Mediums conference started. We were all recently appointed as assistant professors, so we each had a little box of money for doing

Discussion with
Jimenez Lai and **Kristy Balliet**

a conference or a symposium. We did a lot of work to convince our institutions that instead of doing these mini-symposiums at each of our individual schools, it would be better to do a larger event where we could pool together funding across institutions for something like the Possible Mediums event. We ended up convincing four schools: Ohio State University, the University of Chicago, the University of Michigan, and the University of Kentucky. We give a lot of credit to these places and their directors for allowing us to pull that money together.

Mark Foster Gage: That's a huge achievement in itself because most schools operate by saying, if you're going to spend our money on what you're going to do here, we want credit for it. But the fact that you were all so inter-institutional was so important in getting your ideas on the stage. It was really smart to harness all that support in order to broadcast your ideas in a louder register to the architectural world. You needed all that power from all those institutions.

Kristy Balliet: I'll just say one more thing and then hand it over to Jimenez, who is someone we quickly pulled in. We were obsessed with his work and wanted to be in conversation with him. He was teaching in parallel with Kelly Bair at the University of Illinois in Chicago at the time. That's where the workshop component of the conference became important—we were

working on our projects and thinking about the digital and expanding the digital into these other mediums. However, the students we were working with were very much a part of developing that research, as opposed to us having information that we then delivered to the students in a conference. That was the innovative part. So, while the workshop model was not new at that time, the idea that we pulled

Discussion with
Jimenez Lai and **Kristy Balliet**

the conference out of the auditorium and made it a live three-day event, was. The conference, instead, really centered on the workshop and the discourse developed in between the workshop, conference, as well as lunches and dinners. We did expand it to a few other institutions but ultimately it involved about 120 students from those four initial schools. What became important was the idea of shifting from digital technology as an expertise that one would transfer to the students, to the idea that the digital was a territory of exploration that incorporated the students into the research. There's a certain live component of that research that needed to be discussed and shared in real time.

Mark Foster Gage: That's actually something I'd like to double down on, the idea that students make just as valuable a contribution to architectural discourse as the people who are teaching. Gone are the days of a teacher having all of the answers and bequeathing them onto the students. I think a lot of the research that's coming out of architectural institutions is incredibly student-driven, likely due to the tools they have access to. The complex curvature of the TWA terminal project that took Eero Saarinen's office several years to calculate and draw can now be done in an afternoon by most students. Students have been extremely empowered by not only digital tools, but by having access to an unimaginable amount of information. However,

this does sometimes backfire. I was speaking with Mimi Hoang of nARCHITECTS who was conveying how she told a student to look at the work of Josep Lluís Sert, only to return later and have that same student reply, "Yeah, that Sert guy doesn't even have a website." I digress, but I do think you're correct in noting how the conference really leveraged the power of students to participate in and produce discourse in a new way. I also believe it showcased the power that even young faculty can exert on institutions and institutional discourses.

Jimenez Lai: Before I arrived in Chicago, I was teaching at Ohio State University as part of a year-long fellowship slightly before Kristy was there. There are a few schools with a long running successful

Discussion with
Jimenez Lai and **Kristy Balliet**

track record of these kinds of teaching fellowships for young faculty, and I always encourage students to pursue these. The University of Michigan, University of Buffalo, Ohio State University, and Rice University in particular have strong fellowships.

Mark Foster Gage: In addition to the influence of other young faculty and students on your work, has there been a role for mentors other than the aforementioned ones that supported you financially for the Possible Mediums event?

Jimenez Lai: I believe Kristy and I share a few mentor figures. I know José Oubrerie is certainly one of them. I feel like Kristy and I are both, in a way, children of José, who is currently eighty-eight years old.

He's the last man alive that I know of, who worked directly with Le Corbusier. José was thirty-seven or so when Le Corbusier died, and in Le Corbusier's dying days José made him a promise that he would finish the church in Firminy, France that Le Corbusier had designed. That's one of the things I immediately loved about José, how he followed through on a promise to a dying man. Jose finished the Firminy project in 2004, nearly forty years after Le Corbusier had passed.

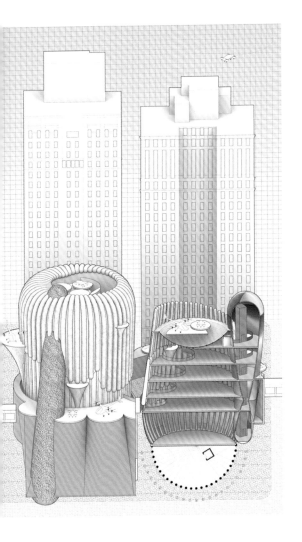

Mark Foster Gage: Jimenez, just for the record, I would like to say as my dying wish that I would like you to finish my Helsinki Guggenheim project after I die. On a more serious note, there's a certain chivalry to José, who I also know a bit. He once told me that he and I were the only people in contemporary architecture to share a Beaux-Arts education. His from the actual École des Beaux-Arts, and mine from the University of Notre Dame, which is the last remaining descendant of that pedagogical system. His is a truly incredible story about dedication and perseverance at the expense of pride and ego. An almost unfathomable concept in our social media age where everyone is the center of the universe and fame is more important than wisdom and self-awareness.

Jimenez Lai: I think what José imparted on me is this feeling of humility and generosity. When you feel like you're out of energy, he still has more. He's incredibly energetic as a teacher and as an architect. At no point in time does he ever throw his hands up in the air and say stuff like, "I'm tired. I'm done." I really admire him. Architecturally, he's somebody who has remained curious even now well into his eighties. He's curious about new

Discussion with
Jimenez Lai and **Kristy Balliet**

technology, new building techniques, and when he's on a review of extremely contemporary work he's able to participate in ongoing conversations. So intelligent. He also reminded me that there's no shame in enjoying formalism and there's no shame in enjoying aesthetics. I came out of school at a time when it would be shameful to like things that look beautiful. I think we're experiencing another time like that right now, where people think just because something is beautiful, it means that the object, or the designer, or the perceiver is shallow.

Mark Foster Gage: We can thank Aristotle via Boethius for that one: this idea that if you look through beauty with x-ray vision, like Lynceus of Argos, you will see the true ugliness inside of a thing. It's a rather large hurdle for aesthetic discourse today to overcome as it has 2,500 years of momentum. However, in the age of Instagram, we can't deny that what we actually see has power, and none of us have the X-ray vision of Lynceus. We need to address the world on the term in which it appears to us, which is why I'm so interested in aesthetic discourse moving beyond that Aristotelian idea.

Jimenez Lai: Right now we are once again in that time period with regards to aesthetics. But José was an old man who told me to not feel bad about my interest in aesthetics. In fact, he noted we might be the last line of defense. If architects don't

care about how the world looks, nobody else is going to. I would also say Jeffrey Kipnis is another mentor figure that we share, as is Greg Lynn. I don't know about Kristy's relationship with Robert Somol, but he was also a really important mentor figure for me as well. When I got to Chicago, I met a few people like Thomas Kelly, Grant Gibson, Stewart Hicks, and we sometimes jokingly spoke about the term the "Midwest Mafia." Then Kyle Miller showed up at the University of Kentucky. Between Chicago, Kentucky, Ohio, and Michigan, a bunch of people were just really bored out of their minds, and it was from within this boredom that this interconnected Midwest-specific discussion came to the surface.

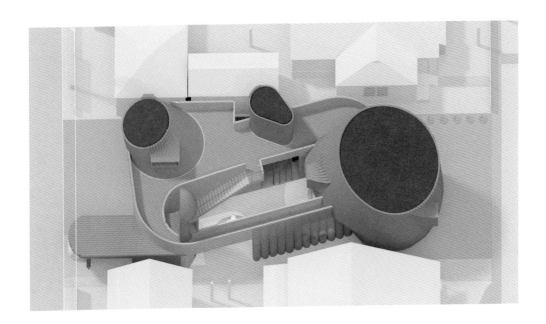

Mark Foster Gage: Jimenez, as someone who was born in the actual Midwest, Nebraska, I cannot convey how offended I was not to have been invited to be part of the Midwest Mafia. You can make it up to me by finishing my Helsinki Guggenheim project.

Jimenez Lai: Your question about influences and mentors reminds me of a story from my time teaching at Ohio State University. One night Andrew Kovacs and I got into a very late, whiskey-filled argument. We paused our debate to turn to our right and realized that Michael Speaks was sitting there at the bar. Coincidentally, Michael was an incredibly important mentor to this Midwest Mafia and the Possible Mediums cohort.

Elise Limon: I wonder if you could talk about the role of film in your work.

Jimenez Lai: I really love films. At UCLA specifically, I helped run a film club where people would get together and talk about films and study unexpected ways to think about the spaces of the film, or the way things were edited. There are certainly spatial implications as to how a film gets cut, for example. There are things we can learn from the contrast of color and atmosphere when we watch films. Usually, when we watch films, we tend to focus on the actor and not the negative spaces around the actor. There were times we would dedicate an entire day to only discussing the spaces around the actor, including the framing and the camera work.

Discussion with
Jimenez Lai and **Kristy Balliet**

We'd look at some of the effects of tilting the camera, focusing the vanishing point at the center of the frame as opposed to shifting the vanishing point to a corner. These discussions went on to shape how I make compositions. Film plays a major role in Bureau Spectacular's work and my teaching. The French word for comic books is bande dessinée, which is related to strips and the predominantly European way of thinking about strips directly translates to something like a film strip. I think these means of storytelling are always in the back of my mind and they find their way into my design work.

Claudia Ansorena: Kristy can you speak to the architect's role in communicating and educating the public about architecture? What kind of mediums might be looked at for that purpose?

Kristy Balliet: Kelly Bair and I have been practicing together for five years as BairBalliet. We started working together on speculative projects, and over the last two and a half years we've been trying to shift the office toward more client-based work. It certainly has prompted a lot of our thinking about what we understand as architects and also how we share that information with our clients. Clients are constantly sending us their Pinterest pages or communicating with us using Instagram saying, "I love this living room." What is fascinating is that it's never the whole living room; it's always just a corner, always just the relationship of a few surfaces essentially.

Mark Foster Gage: I would say one thing that really differentiates my peers from your peers is that we never wanted our

architecture to be or look easy. We needed to have a complexity and one needed to understand the deep mathematical concepts behind the work. An example of this was our collective interest in the nature of topological surfaces, which is something that comes from Greg Lynn, who we all have been influenced by in one way or another. I would say the people in orbit of Possible Mediums were a little bit more in the Robert Somol school of thought, where form didn't need to be difficult or complex. His idea of "shape" as to Greg Lynn's ideas of "form" posited that it's okay for architecture to be easy, fun, and consumable.

I've listened to some of the words you use when you describe your work Kristy, you use terms like "cute" and "play" and "swivel." Jimenez has described things he has done as "sassy" and "lazy" and as "characters." These are things that are easy to understand, and I can see how that's liberating in terms of having freedom as a designer, but why is it better for architecture to be easy and consumable as opposed to challenging?

Kristy Balliet: Kelly typically introduces me as someone who has a proclivity for complexity and I introduced her as

Discussion with
Jimenez Lai and **Kristy Balliet**

someone who is interested in legibility, clarity, sharpness. She's incredibly witty and I'm much nerdier. It goes back and forth.

Mark Foster Gage: You can see that in your collaborative work too. Of the Possible Mediums group, I would say your work uses the most complex three-dimensional surfaces and is the most geometrically complex. It relies heavily on the computer. It's interesting to hear you describe that as kind of a tug of war between these polls within your practice.

Kristy Balliet: I still bristle at client Pinterest pages, but Kelly is more open to embracing this and thinking about how our work can be accessible to multiple audiences. I am always trying to sneak in a little more volumetric or geometric moments that are a bit more difficult. For instance, I would never want to do a pure extrusion, I'm always going to look for a way to make it swivel a little bit.

Mark Foster Gage: Pure extrusion is a good lead in to a question for Jimenez. Mr. Pure Extrusion. Considering that the language of cartoons can be understood as a human vernacular that goes back at least 60,000 years to the oldest of the existing cave paintings, you would be the poster child for the opposite end of the spectrum that Kelly is describing. With the possible exception of Andrew Kovacs, your work is among the funnest of the fun, and the flattest of the flat. It's unapologetically easily consumable. Talk.

Jimenez Lai: That line between difficult and easy is something that I've been thinking about for years. I'll use a comparison between two artists who exemplify this contrast. Someone like Vincent van Gogh, for example, wants the audience to see every last brush stroke. He is looking to make the process evident, making sure that it's clear how difficult this is, and maybe even in the process communicating his pains, struggles, and the anguish of each stroke. The contrast is someone like Roy Lichtenstein, who appears as the total opposite. The process is almost entirely concealed. Unless you get up really, really close you can't tell how the paint was applied. Although it wasn't, it might

as well have been digitally printed. There's smoothness and ease that conveys the lack of effort and pain, but it doesn't mean that the work is easy to make. In fact, Lichtenstein's work is probably just as difficult or maybe even more difficult to produce as you can't hide any errors like you can in a van Gogh. This translates to architecture, for instance, when we think about drywall. You have to be really skilled if you want the drywall to be smooth and flat and well painted so that it goes almost unnoticed. That type of ease comes with both skill and technique. Maybe this comes from my move from Chicago to Los Angeles to teach at UCLA. In Chicago people complain as a sport, whereas in LA it's almost as though people are sparing each other the pain of complaining and the attitude is to just chill and take it easy. The chill attitude is something that I've decided to adopt as a form of generosity, sparing others from complaint. Not just personally but also compositionally.

Mark Foster Gage: Your work is very chill, and increasingly LA. That is also funny, because I interviewed Tom Wiscombe, who is of course in LA as well, and he was talking about his new monograph. I said that you can always tell when a book is written by someone from Los Angeles because the font is so big that you don't have to do much reading. It's that same chill generosity you're talking about, sparing people from having to read. I suppose it's

Discussion with
Jimenez Lai and **Kristy Balliet**

The Tower vacuumed all nearby resources and population. Architecture became the city.

This reversed the figure-ground relationship between Manhattan and the Central Park.

The government implemented all public spaces and amenities inside the tower, drawing a zoning map in an architectural section. It made sense for citizens to abandon suburbia.

my elitist, New York City, Ivy League, sushi-eating, liberal tendencies that bristles at creative practice being or looking easy. I'm always drawn to the extremely difficult. It's similar to how Rachmaninoff had huge hands, so his compositions are very difficult for mere mortals to play. I suppose Rachmaninoff isn't too big in LA.

Saba Salekfard: How does the role of narrative play out in your work? What kind of subjects are you constructing with your architecture? Secondly, you discussed the space between irony and sincerity. Could you speak more about that?

Jimenez Lai: This also leads back to the previous question about my interest in cinema. In terms of thinking about narrative, it's through cartoons. In a way, when we build things, we are building sets.

Mark Foster Gage: Very Shakespearean. As if pulled directly from *As You like It*: "All the world's a stage, and all the men and women are merely players."

Jimenez Lai: I've always been convinced that the set is doing just as much work in defining a character as the acting. If we think of historic paintings of saints, the aura glowing around them becomes part of their character.

Mark Foster Gage: I know we share an interest in how architecture produces curiosity, albeit in a different register. Can you tie together the easy and the philosophical?

I am always drawn to people who are curious about philosophy.

Jimenez Lai: I personally am curious about philosophy, and I believe if we think of architecture as a construction of reality, then the questioning of reality allows for collaborative conversations between philosophers and architects. I know someone from the University of Oslo, his name is Timotheus Vermeulen, and he's more of a cultural theorist and philosopher. He usually works with art, film, and literary critics. We've come to a kind of agreement that architecture seems to be a bit slower than some of these other creative mediums. For instance, it took architecture until the 1980s to recognize itself as postmodern, whereas if you look at cinema and literature that happened a lot quicker and a lot earlier. I think the architects who were doing postmodernism perhaps didn't know that they were doing it at the time, but the recognition came later. Much later than in most other disciplines. So, for me to think about where we are might be impossible in the same way, we'll only find out later. From my point of view, I'm just producing an ongoing body of work and simultaneously observing the body of work of my peers. At the moment, I'm interested in that oscillation between irony and sincerity and putting irony inside sincerity. It is just somehow for me in the air and in my work.

Mark Foster Gage: Kristy. Do you want to talk about narrative or irony and sincerity in your work?

Kristy Balliet: This is where Jimenez and I probably have the most difference. Narrative does not play a large role in our work or how it is developed. We certainly think about relationships between multiple objects, or the relationships between subject and object. One could think of these relationships as our version of the story of the architecture that we're developing. We are constantly working on designing the spaces between architecture as much as we are the architecture itself. Maybe this is similar to what Jimenez is referring to in his interest in the negative space in film. I think that comes a lot from my obsession with volume, paired with Kelly's obsession with a sort of graphic profile. We also

talk about our work in terms of "character," albeit to a different degree, but I think that there might be some crossover with Jimenez as well. I think about things like how a building stretches, how it stands on its tiptoes, and I begin to give the building a character in my mind as I am working on it. I'll have thoughts like, "Oh that's too aggressive," or "That's too earnest." I don't know if it's quite as posture driven as Jimenez, but there's definitely overlap. The way that this might contribute to narrative would come back to relationships.

Mark Foster Gage: One of the things I've noticed is that architecture schools now, and rightfully so, are beginning to address questions of social justice and equality in both the way the profession works and in what it produces. However, I worry that some practices are becoming marginalized

Discussion with
Jimenez Lai and **Kristy Balliet**

172

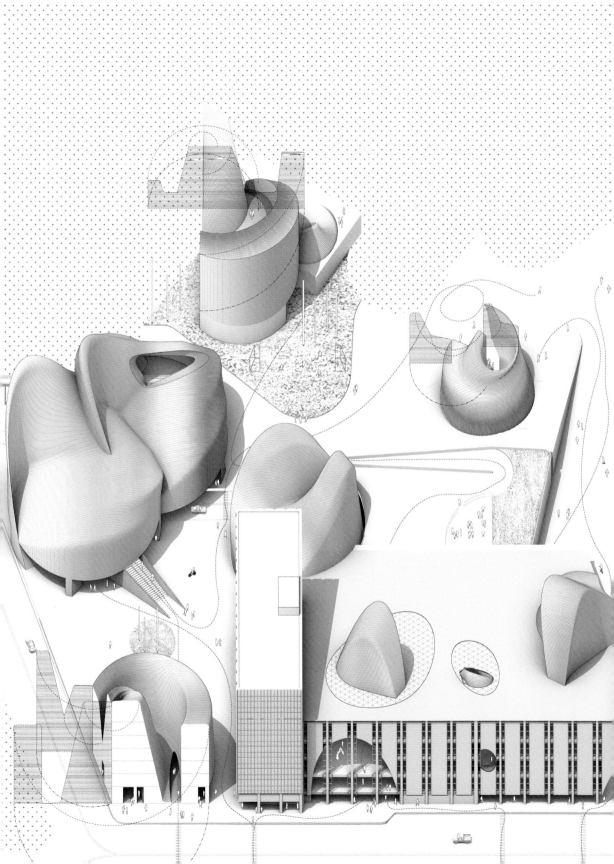

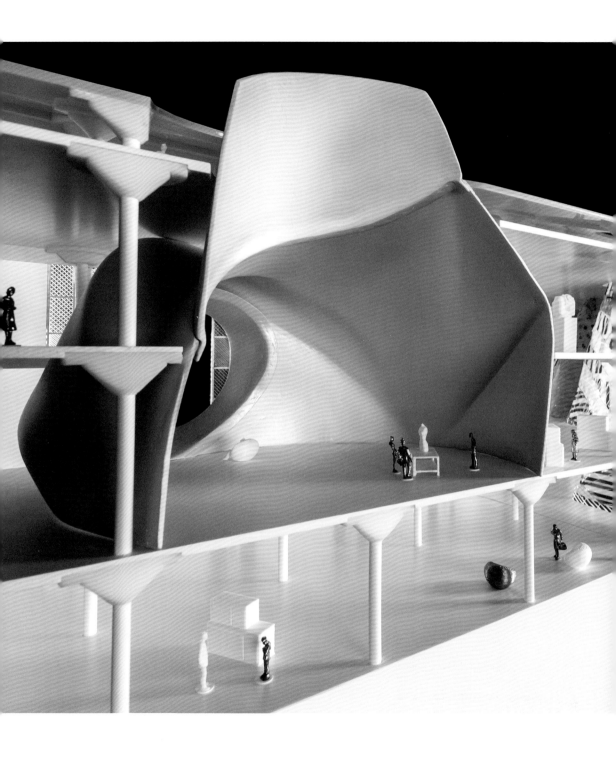

Discussion with
Jimenez Lai and **Kristy Balliet**

because they didn't shift immediately to show how their work was addressing these issues. How do you think architecture can or should address questions of social justice? How do you think architects can continue to work on the ideas they've dedicated to researching, while also working on folding in these increasingly foregrounded social concerns? And what do you think the timescale of that folding is?

Jimenez Lai: I think about the Korean architect Minsuk Cho all the time. He's one of my favorite architects, and I really admire his work. His work is beautiful and he has built a lot of amazing buildings. His construction techniques are really fantastic, and he worked at OMA for a decade so he's also extremely talented at programming a building. He knows all that, and does all that, but what do I really admire about him? He hangs around the City Hall and he talks to politicians in order to get to know them. He doesn't do this to get himself projects, but more to whisper ideas to them that would benefit the welfare of his fellow Koreans. Over time, these whispers become actual architectural or urban actions. In a sense, he is a stealth advisor to the political class in Korea. I am just so amazed at his ability to navigate politics and do something good in addition to being such a great architect who, despite all of this additional political engagement, still doesn't sacrifice aesthetics or the quality of construction in his work. I admire that.

Mark Foster Gage: That's one thing that José Oubrerie was trying to convey when he taught you that you don't have to apologize for having a formal interest. It's just that people assume if you do have a formal interest, that you don't have a social interest. I think that's a false opposition.

Kristy Balliet: Some people are able to move quickly in their practice and shift their passion architecturally toward these issues, but in other instances architects can also be a significant part of culture as citizens. Another way that I think I can contribute to these issues is to think about how I teach architecture and how I talk about architecture. The things I choose to read now are very different from what I was reading five years ago. All of those shifts are in progress for me, as a citizen. I very much see myself as a part of that conversation and I'm educating myself. This impacts the way I think about architecture and the way I work within it.

Mark Foster Gage: We can exert our political influence as architects in a way that's not always directly through architecture or design itself.

Jimenez Lai: Right. He doesn't stand on a soapbox and say, "This is bad, we can't have this," but he is still helping. Again, I use the word stealth. It takes someone to observe someone else's work closely to know this is happening because he doesn't make his work about that. However, if you look close enough and listen closely enough to what he does, you realize that he is somebody who slowly turns the oil tanker without anyone noticing.

Mark Foster Gage: I appreciate the emphasis on self-education about these issues that are only now being so dramatically illuminated for us as citizens and architects. I always worry about architecture's knee-jerk reaction that it can fix things. For instance, during the refugee crisis there were a bunch of architects designing refugee housing, although it was all entirely unrealistic to think it would be built and actually help solve the problem. Sometimes our profession has the tendency to promote

Discussion with
Jimenez Lai and **Kristy Balliet**

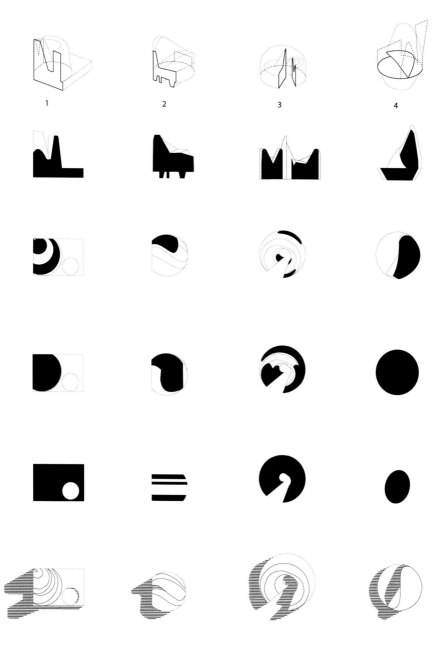

1   2   3   4

Discussion with
Jimenez Lai and **Kristy Balliet**

the idea that "we have the answers, we can fix this!" I think questions of social justice really need to be absorbed over time and not faux-immediately solved by architecture and architects. It always comes across as the worst kind of white or professional saviorism.

Kristy Balliet: This is where we absolutely are all peers, in our need to reeducate ourselves in terms of the things that we were taught as students versus what we should be teaching our own students.

Mark Foster Gage: In our disciplinary idea of historic cannon, not only the voices that were championed when we were students, but also the voices that were excluded from such championing are all fertile territory for us to reconsider the operational lore we inherited. We have to keep in mind the fictional tendencies of history.

Vicky Achnani: Architecture is something that is highly layered in terms of function, form, space, experience. These things make up one side of practice. The other side might be described as the methods used by an architect to design or produce their discourse. In your case, the latter has been through stories, models, speculation, etc. How do you develop these in tandem? Do you delay one due to another?

Kristy Balliet: It's reasonable that our projects have different priorities. We have actively tried to keep within the office multiple parallel projects happening at the same time, some of them being more client-based and some of them being more about discourse. Some day that may change. Ironically, we met with Hernán Díaz Alonso, the director of SCI-Arc, about moving forward with a virtual version of our exhibition design in the SCI-Arc gallery on the same day that we signed a contract with a local Boys and Girls Club to work on a renovation for them. There was definitely a time a few years ago as a practice, we would have said, "I think we can't do the Boys and Girls Club right now, we need to really focus on this larger speculative project." It was a very important moment in our practice for us to sign that Boys and Girls Club contract knowing that we had to gear up the office in a more professional way. We need to be able to move back and forth between these separate client-based and conceptual conversations that were, literally, happening on the same day. That's one way that we are trying to develop our mental agility, to be able to move across these interests within architecture and do work for multiple audiences.

Jimenez Lai: For lack of a better word, I think the word omnivore describes what we do at Bureau Spectacular. We consume a lot of things, we digest a lot of things, and we produce a lot of things. I feel like it's just what we are, as a profession, we are omnivores.

Pop, Color, and Supergraphics

Discussion with
Elena Manferdini and **Florencia Pita**
of Studio Manferdini and
Florencia Pita & Co.

screen proliferation and social media,
Instagram as the new Las Vegas, technology
and supergraphics, color and desire,
the democratization of color

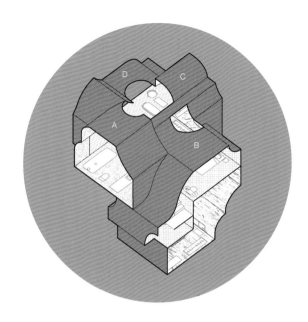

Mark Foster Gage: The discursive topics I had in mind were ones that you are both absolutely pioneering in, particularly in the large-scale use of color, patterns, and graphics in architecture. This is a discourse with very little background in 20th-century architectural practices, most of whom were convinced that the absence of these elements brought the building closer to an internationally accessible purity. Adolph Loos went so far as to call ornamentation a crime, and this included the "unnecessary" use of graphics and patterns. Aside from simply creating beautiful work, you both play a part in the rediscovery of how architects can use graphics and patterns in sophisticated and contemporary ways.

Elena Manferdini: There have been areas of overlap between Florencia's work and my work throughout the years. I think this conversation will be a great opportunity to discuss some commonalities and differences concerning our shared interests.

Florencia Pita: I want to not only have a conversation about graphics in terms of "supergraphics," but also touch upon graphics as a study on geometry and a study of lines. Specifically, I'd like to start by discussing the latter. This is best shown in the work of figures like the Swiss graphic designer, Armin Hofmann. In his work you find yourself understanding the elements of graphics, through dots, lines, gradation, and patterns. I'm particularly interested in the reading of graphics as lines. What is interesting to see in Hofmann's work, is his moves toward a tectonic understanding of the line as a thick concrete element. In a way, the line becomes a supergraphic that can interact with the architecture. A great example of this can be found in the work of a student of Hofmann, Barbara Stauffacher Solomon. Her painted interiors for the Sea Ranch were designed through a process of sketching, extracting, and prolonging lines of the existing building. In that project, we can see how the building and the graphics start to work together. Conversely, when I think of supergraphics I tend to think about the work of Ray and Charles Eames. They didn't just see their work simply for its fabrication elements or its material qualities within the post war landscape. They also looked at their work as supergraphics, understanding their work as having both two- and three-dimensional qualities.

Mark Foster Gage: Do you think that the way you use colors and graphics are new to the field? How do you think your work differs from how color has been used in the past? The ultimate way to phrase this question is, do you think that there's some emerging sensibility related to color and pattern that is endemic to our moment in history?

Elena Manferdini: Historically colors have been a silent but powerful protagonist of architectural production. During specific architectural periods the presence of color has been denied, while in other instances color has invaded the architectural canvas. Looking at our recent times, the rise of social media has democratized the sharing of images, and with it the sharing of colorful images of architecture. Social media has propelled a wide trafficking of images of architecture and with it has created an audience that consider colors as attractive. Social media has provided access to a full spectrum of colors, and with it has also propelled a desire for new chromatic sensibilities. As was the case for the early Modernists, there is no longer a single spectrum of colors one can use in architecture. The digital turn made us realize that a much wider set of possibilities should enter and break the canons of

Discussion with
Elena Manferdini and **Florencia Pita**

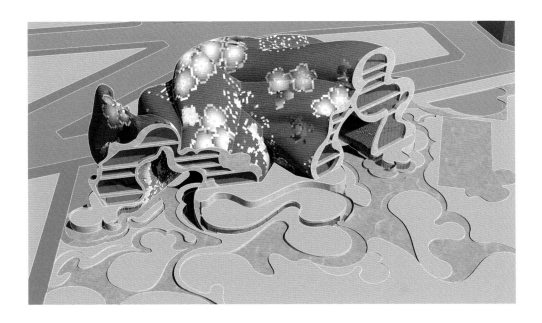

the past. The architect's primary design medium has become a computer, and more specifically, colors started inhabiting the computer screen. It's imperative to note that the essence of the medium we work with is colored light. The fact that a designer can make changes to a shader in a modeling program—or change those material effects—fuels a new appetite for color. We not only design with digital colors, but these images are then disseminated through a series of flat screens like our smart phones, tablets, and monitors. So, in both the computer and the social media disseminating images, colored light becomes integral to producing and consuming the image. This is a new way of receiving and understanding color. Color

has come to represent a variety of tastes, identities, people, and genders. Color now represents many more ideas than it has historically. Color is subjective. Color exists in the eye of the beholder, and the beholder of today is diverse. Today we are finally coming to terms that diversity is a cultural and social richness. Our use of color today reflects this fundamental shift in society. In addition to that, it is interesting to see how social media has fueled the desire

Discussion with
Elena Manferdini and **Florencia Pita**

for chromatic spaces, and such desire has moved from the internet into architecture and then back to the digital image, posted and shared. During the past few years we have witnessed the proliferation of vibrant chromatic physical experiences, a so-called Instagram-friendly architecture. Social media has instigated the desire for a new genre of spaces, namely pop-ups, which are designed to be imageable, and shareable on social media. Yet these spaces are not designed to be permanent in the way that architecture historically has been. The function of these experiences is to act as a background for the imagination, for acting, for posing, for selfies of a diverse society. The method of dissemination is built into the space. Color has entered architecture and in a dramatic new way.

Mark Foster Gage: Architecture is being consumed as an image on Instagram as much as it is a building in real space, and color allows that real space to play a more important role within this social media milieu. It's a really interesting idea. I also think what you said about designing through light is important, how the vibrancy we have access to is greater than any group of architects have had access to in human history. Colored pencils on a piece of paper, for example, very literally pales in comparison to looking at an Illustrator document on your screen that has a million colors that are all backlit with illuminating light. You also described a level of

Discussion with
Elena Manferdini and **Florencia Pita**

accessibility in the way that we experience color; There's no barrier to enjoying color today because we're inundated with it on our screens. It makes me think of how rare and expensive some colors used to be. A great example is the use of purple for emperors in Rome, and how people would have very rarely seen designed objects that were purple. Similarly, in the Renaissance the main source for blue paint was crushed up lapis lazuli. That stone was incredibly expensive, so seeing artificial blue in a painting was super rare. Now we use purples and blues with reckless abandon because they're no more difficult to produce than ochres and umbers, which have historically been cheaper. There is now a democracy to color that did not exist in the past, and I think that democratizing ability carries over to its use in architecture. It's something that can be enjoyed without necessarily relying on a concept. Color is something that everyone understands intuitively and can enjoy intuitively.

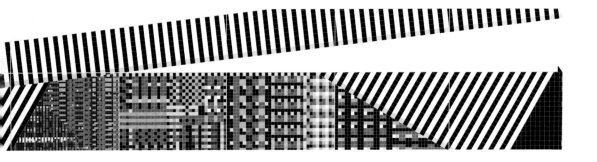

Elena Manferdini: Color has a different meaning within everyone's individual and cultural histories, so it can also become a proxy for a battleground of ideas; an example of this is race or gender. I don't think the use of color is superficial or frivolous, colors are able to trigger responses in audiences that are much more complex than what we can predict as architects. It provides a portal to a conversation with a much more variegated group of spectators. Color does not exist per se. The way I see color is different from how you see color, which is different from my screen, which is different from your screen. Suddenly we understand that something invisible is visible only through the audience. Color, as such, can and has been a catalyst for change within our culture. In the past, the architect's creativity has been confined by a sense of chromophobia. Today, we can use the entire chromatic spectrum, and we are now asked to confront the desire for those colors and their uses. We also asked to reproduce digital colors into a physical reality, which is an exciting but difficult

task. This is the post-optic problem; how do you produce effects that you've never seen in reality, but you experience through the computer screen? How do you produce reality based on a different kind of vision?

Mark Foster Gage: How do you link these ideas up with how color has been used throughout architectural history?

Discussion with
Elena Manferdini and **Florencia Pita**

Florencia Pita: If you look at the work of Denise Scott Brown, there was a discovery and an emphasis on the world of images in advertising and signage that nobody in architecture cared about. By introducing them into architecture she produced new ideas about the use of color and super-graphics. This parallels art's relationship with the advent of the printed image, so you started to see supergraphics in the form of advertisements on the sides of build-ings making cities much more colorful. Buildings became colorful because they had a Coca Cola ad, or they had a giant man or woman on the side of a building. Ads started to introduce color at an architectur-al scale into cities without the architecture itself being colorful. Elena and I have been

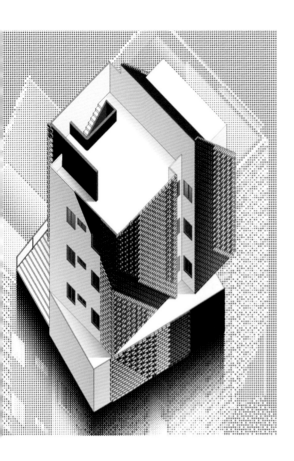

applying a color to something just to have a signifier. I believe that the use of color in architecture should convert your experience of certain spaces, not merely be used as a backdrop for a drawing.

Mark Foster Gage: I think the word you mentioned, "immersiveness," is an important one. It contrasts the way a postmodern architect like Michael Graves used color, where he would have a building made of a cube, a cylinder and a pyramid. The pyramid would be blue, the cylinder would be orange, and cube would be yellow. It's a coding of geometry, where each piece receives one color. I think the ways you both have been using color is much more complex. Immersive coloration goes way beyond simply coding geometry. As you've matured into two architects that have very specific types of practices and architectural projects that you're very well known for, were there key moments or people in your education or practice that you encountered? What were the flashbulbs that made you such colorful architects?

Elena Manferdini: There are many people whose work has been influential to me in the past. The experience of working for Greg Lynn was pivotal in shaping my relationship with digital tools. Sylvia Lavin was also a significant influence in my life, as was being in Los Angeles while Frank Gehry's WDCH was under construction. However, when you detach yourself from those mentorships, the real

working with color for many years and I think we have focused more on exposing it rather than theorizing it. Now everyone is using more adventurous colors in their renderings, in their images, and in the backgrounds of their drawings. As an architect or architecture student, why do you need a colored background for your drawing? What happened? I always thought that color in architecture had to do with immersion and with full experience, not simply

work starts. When you become an individual, and you understand that you have your own argument and your own project, that's the moment when the real journey starts. When it comes to color, one of the greatest influences for me was my upbringing in a different country where painting and colorful architecture is everywhere. At times I consider myself an artist, a painter through the medium of architecture.

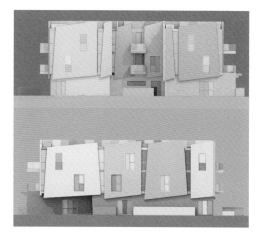

Florencia Pita: I worked for Peter Eisenman right after my undergraduate program, and later worked for Greg Lynn. For graduate school I went to Columbia University and consider myself lucky to have been taught by Sanford Kwinter. Isn't it interesting how all of those people that I mentioned are all white men? I think that each person has to be very aware of who your mentors are. What is your dialogue with your mentor? Who do you choose to be your mentor? So I want to place emphasis on somebody like Sylvia Lavin, who was the most influential person in regard to many of the things that I have done in my practice. Her book *Flash in the Pan* has been particularly resourceful to me. It's a really small book that addresses much of what we've been discussing, including color. So there are direct mentors, but then there are the other mentors, those I have specifically chosen, such as Anni Albers and Ray Eames. Not Josef or Charles.

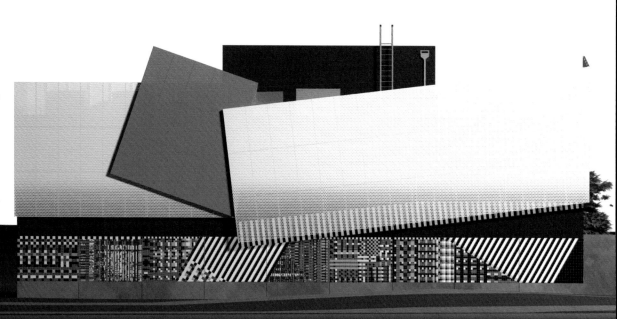

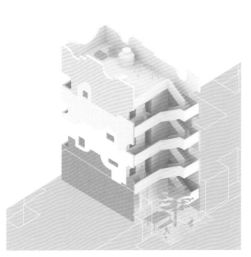 

Samar Halloum: From my experience, color is typically referred to when a client says they want something to be "Instagrammable." That's what you usually hear from clients and that's where you end up adding color to elements. It's completely different than thinking about color as a three-dimensional or spatial experience. I'm curious if you think that this is taking color's relationship with architecture in a positive direction, or do you think it's influencing it in a negative way?

Elena Manferdini: To say that an Instagramable use of color is superficial is true, but not in a negative way. Nowadays color is the most powerful tool in the box. Color has the ability to make something attractive, while creating a feedback loop between author and audience. The desire for color fuels the will to reproduce it in the physical world. When this process comes full circle it doesn't mean that the loop is closed. Social media continually loops the audience into the mix. For the first time, it's not just the architect and the client making decisions but a larger audience. Social media is a democratizing force that opened up design to a wider audience that is now part of the creative process. Having an audience that enjoys something to such an extent that it influences the sensibility of design is part of what we need to address as architects today. It doesn't mean that, as architects, we have become superficial. It just means that we can have a much broader spectrum of options and opinions to work with as architects. This is liberating in terms of what architects can do, and that is precisely where issues of

Discussion with
Elena Manferdini and **Florencia Pita**

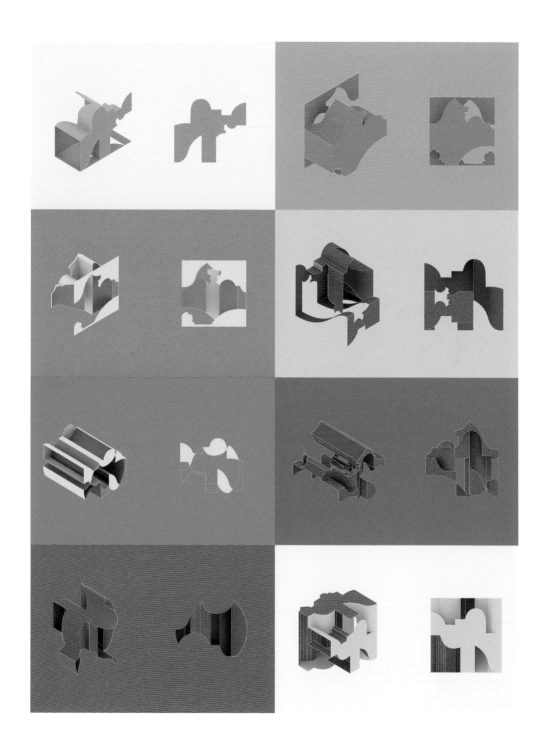

gender, race, and politics come into play. The speed at which we're consuming architecture, consuming images, consuming colors, consuming superficial ideas about color is extremely powerful. It brings to the table many more voices than were heard in architecture's past.

Mark Foster Gage: One usually hears architects lamenting the influence of Instagram on architecture, for making it superficial or consumable. However, it may be that very quality that we would have previously called superficial that allows for a much larger audience to participate in architecture. Historically, it has been a fairly elitist profession that spotlights the people in power.

Florencia Pita: I have mixed feelings about a reappraisal of superficiality. About thirteen years ago, you and I guest-edited the 17th issue of *Log*. We called it the "superficial issue" to make a point and put it on the table as a subject. We wanted to produce conversations about the role of superficiality in architecture, in both the literal sense and the metaphorical sense. It allowed us to introduce into architectural discourse topics like feelings, emotion, and a cultural value of "flashes in the pan" to borrow the phrase from Sylvia Lavin.

Mark Foster Gage: It was 2009 when we guest-edited that *Log* issue, right around the time social media became the cultural phenomenon that we have today. That

Discussion with
Elena Manferdini and **Florencia Pita**

issue anticipated Instagram and the issues it would raise.

Florencia Pita: Again, I have mixed feelings regarding social media. Yesterday I was "on site" virtually, with a client who was taking selfies in West Hollywood in front of a building that will eventually have an "Instagram facade." This morning I was using those selfies to develop that facade. I mean, I'll design it. I'm a designer. I will design whatever is necessary as long as it's creative. Who knows what the medium might be in ten years? In any case, the building will still be standing there. I do see the potential in Instagram, if we see it through the lens of *Learning from Las Vegas* we could imagine it producing similar research and a subsequent impact on architecture.

Mark Foster Gage: So, the issue of Instagram in architecture hasn't been properly theorized and needs to go through a *Learning from Las Vegas* type of process to be folded into the discipline more intelligently?

Florencia Pita: I don't know. Elena's positive attitude about Instagram is true to a degree, and yet there is a lot of negative commenting on that platform. Sure, you don't have a "dislike" button, but I've read some pretty horrible things in the comments that would make me prefer a "dislike" button. It is a culture of the many, but it is also a culture of anonymity, a culture

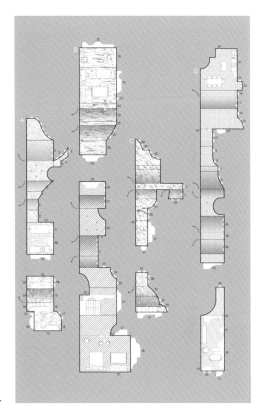

of "them." The dark side of Instagram makes me a little bit conflicted with this positivism. It has a positive and a negative impact. It's the world we're in, and we have to work with our world. I'm obviously conflicted. I don't have an answer to the social media reality, but it's what we have. It's like Las Vegas. You can say Las Vegas was horrific when Denise Scott Brown went there, but in asking what we could learn from Las Vegas, architecture did pick up quite a bit. The same thing will happen with Instagram, eventually.

Mark Foster Gage: That issue of *Log* we guest-edited was the first one that incorporated color into the cover. The first ten issues of *Log* were all white and the second ten issues of *Log* we're all black. Within that black series we had a riotously colorful illustration of an explosion on it, that you could view with accompanying 3D glasses. It was as if to say, "We're here, and there's something new in discourse." The word superficial was a pejorative used to dismiss things like aesthetics and color and textures so we took that word and said "let's resurrect the superficial and see what we can learn from it," again, like Las Vegas. You actually can't buy the *Log* #17 issue anymore because the artist, a friend of mine at the time, Tristan Eaton has since become rather famous. It sells for around USD 1,000 if you can find it.

Florencia Pita: One thing you didn't mention was that we did that issue right after the economy totally collapsed. These massive societal changes are opportunities to look at the world differently. We are headed that direction again in 2022 as we assess what happened with COVID and how it impacted the world.

Ingrid Liu: What role does media play in your design process? I see a distinction in both of your practices between projects driven by color, and projects driven by monochromatic patterns. Taking Elena's work for example, the spatial design is more colorful while the jewelry is monochromatic. The fabric and textile work is

colorful, yet the fashion design is monochromatic. Is there a tendency to subconsciously create a syntax with how you work across different project scales?

Elena Manferdini: Architects are generalists, and I say this in the best possible way. It's an education that allows us to work in many design fields. That is a richness rather than a constraint. This means that we can dive into the design at different scales and in different design fields. On the topic of a generalist approach to practice, what can't be glossed over is the utility of software packages. Like color, technology becomes a crucial democratizing force when developers lower the level of expertise needed to use certain tools. When software becomes more user-friendly, you can export your skills within many different design fields. I love to cross boundaries in my practice, It holds my interests and passion. A software shared by many design fields allows architects to branch out. For instance, architects can design at different scales, spanning from the scale of a building to the scale of jewelry. Being a technological generalist will enable you to rethink form in ways you aren't allowed to think about in architecture. What happens when the ground is a dynamic body that moves three-dimensionally? You must think about ground as something completely different. Architecture makes us think in one way. You have a ground and you think about gravity. The computer suddenly allows you to say, "Well, what if the ground is the human body?" Suddenly your relationship to shape must change.

Ninth Chapter

Aesthetics and Architecture in High Resolution

Discussion with
Mark Foster Gage and **Claude Rains**
of Mark Foster Gage Architects

*curiosity and complexity, brute-force design:
the efforts of iteration, hybrid intelligence,
speculative realism's entry into architecture*

Claude Rains: Where does your fascination in complexity come from and what sustains it?

Mark Foster Gage: I get that question a lot; why make work so difficult and complex? Let me start to answer this by saying I don't want anyone else to do my work; my goal is not to get people to copy me. I don't need the competition, and the work of our office is very labor intensive. It's also generally a terrible business model, because the more money you spend on design the less profit you make if you are using a standard architectural billing method. So right off the bat, you can tell my practice is not one dedicated solely to

the idea of profit, growth, or world domination. This is just a fact, as far as business is concerned. It would be much easier if we were minimalists. We live in a world where minimalism is almost a vernacular. The absence of qualities is often mistaken for great design. It's why I have and use, but don't like, the design of iPhones. They are nearly always objects without visual qualities. It's absolutely not designed to fit in your hand, it's slippery, sleek, and designed to look good in photos. I land on the opposite spectrum from the iPhone, which has me more interested in complex details, textures, colors, patterns, and the aspects of design that oppose minimalism, at least in aesthetic terms.

Claude Rains: How does this supposed burden of higher levels of complexity translate to the design process in your office?

Mark Foster Gage: We work in a system of iterations, meaning that we don't design something to look a certain way, we design it and then ask if it looks that certain way. We then ask how we can make it look more the way we want it to look. We design it again, then design it again, and then we'll pick the one that looks best or meets the kind of aesthetic criteria we have, after which we'll design ten more and pick the best, design ten more and pick the best, etc. We throw away almost all of our work, as we'll easily go through ninety-nine iterations of something to find the one we'll use. For instance, we're doing a book on a single project right now, which includes about 1,700 images that we didn't use. In a competition, you may present ten rendered images. To produce those ten final images, we went through 1,700 other images to get there.

Claude Rains: How would you describe the role that software serves in the production of your work?

Mark Foster Gage: We don't do everything in one software program that we're all expert in, it's actually the reverse. None of us are actually very good at a particular

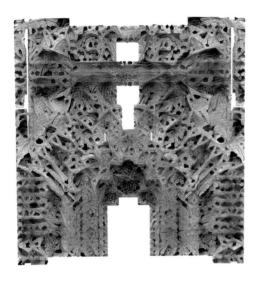

software program. We're just willing to put in the time to experiment with many different programs and see what comes out. We change the primary software programs we use every few years as a result of this. The reason I'm interested in doing that is because the type of software, and the way we use software, is a form of innovation within the profession. It's a way of developing not only new techniques, and new formal languages, but also new ways of imbuing contemporary form with a historic flavor or historic relevance. We don't recognize, as other architects do, the existence of any deep divide between classical, historical, or contemporary formal languages. Nothing is off-limits, and everything in particular within architectural history is "fair game" as we aim toward innovation. One can absolutely innovate

with history. This belief largely comes from my background as a classical architect. I was trained in classical architecture, so I have a particular knowledge of history. That being said, I don't have a particular deep knowledge of 20th-century architecture. This is actually kind of interesting because I did my undergraduate studies focusing entirely on classical architecture. When I went to Yale I started doing the most high-end digital stuff around the year 2000, so I essentially skipped the 20th century. This provides a good explanation for why my work looks the way it does. I'm more or less allergic to minimalism, it's just not my sensibility. My life would be much easier if I loved minimalism. It just seems so much faster and easier to design.

Taiga Taba: Could you talk a bit about Object Oriented Ontology and how that philosophy plays a role in your projects?

Mark Foster Gage: I came across Graham Harman's work maybe around 2014, a bit after it started to come into architecture, midwifed by David Ruy. At the time the dominant discourse in architecture was Parametricism and I was never part of that discourse. Patrik Schumacher, the late Zaha Hadid's design partner, was the champion of the theoretical position behind parametric design, which I always thought was rather weak. Essentially it was based around this idea of using a digital surface to incorporate thousands of different components that are all interrelated—para-metrics, adjacent metrics, or adjacent measurements. That specific architectural language placed importance on interconnectivity. Every component was linked, via the computer, to each other, and in Patrik's position, to social relationships. It's interesting conceptually because it allows you to think of architecture as connections of interrelationships, but it doesn't give you the ability to talk about the building as a singular thing that has a cultural impact of its own. The theory is predicated entirely on interconnectivity rather than discrete objects. Everybody at the time was talking about interconnectivity this and interconnectivity that, both in architecture but also in philosophy via the lingering presence of Deleuze. For instance, one of Deleuze's ideas is that things don't exist in a stable form but that they're always in the process of becoming something. Deleuze might say that a can of Coke is not a can of Coke, but that it is actually just aluminum that's on its way from being something in the ground to being recycled and becoming a computer part or ending up in a landfill. You would use the trajectory of a timeline to say that a Coke can is not a discrete object, but rather that it is an instance of aluminum somewhere in its lifespan from start to finish. This is really interesting because it allows us to think about time, but doesn't really work if we want to talk about discrete objects like buildings, and their impact on culture. Deleuze doesn't allow for

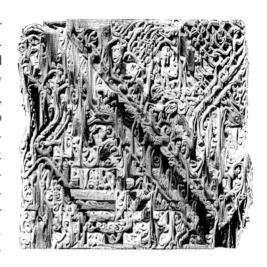

buildings to exist as discrete object, they are only collections of materials on their way to becoming something else. Such Deleuzian description of the object places the emphasis on the process within a larger timeline, rather than emphasizing objects in the world. Object-Oriented Ontology, or OOO for short, emerged in philosophy around 2008 and said, "no wait a minute, this IS a can of Coke. We have a word for it: can. I'm holding it, it is actually an object, it may have a past and it may have a future, but its past and its future are mostly removed from one's current experience." OOO makes the case that we can relate to an object most effectively as humans by addressing them in the present, through their currently existing aesthetic qualities. With a can of Coke, one can never access all of its past, or can never access all of its future. What OOO gave architects in that era of interconnectivity was the ability to pause and look at a discrete object and think about it for its own qualities; in particular, its own aesthetic qualities.

Claude Rains: Your description of the relationship between aesthetic qualities and perception favors the present. How does that relationship differ in terms of an object's past or future?

Mark Foster Gage: Graham Harman might say that an apple is an apple and it has aesthetic qualities that orbit it, metaphorically. Let's continue with the apple analogy. An apple has a core, no pun intended, of apple-ness. There is something about an apple that makes it an apple. Its aesthetic qualities, some of which you can see, some of which you have no access to, some of which are stable, and some of which change. So we have a discrete object that is capable of addressing appearances in the world, being addressed in the present, but also capable of addressing change. Sometimes that apple is red, sometimes the apple is green, but eventually green fades and red comes in as it ripens. The change from green to red doesn't change the fact that it's an apple. Therefore, some aesthetic qualities are things that come and go. Some of these qualities have particular meanings to us as humans, and some do not. In our office we're interested in trying to develop new aesthetic qualities in buildings that have not existed before; blue apples, as it were. We're interested in

our projects having meaning in the present moment rather than thinking about their past life or their life in the far-away future. This doesn't discount thinking about sustainability, or other important aspects like that. We have absolutely no interest in architecture because of its concepts. So if I say, for instance, "my design for a building is based on an octagon because there are eight religions in my country. It's a good

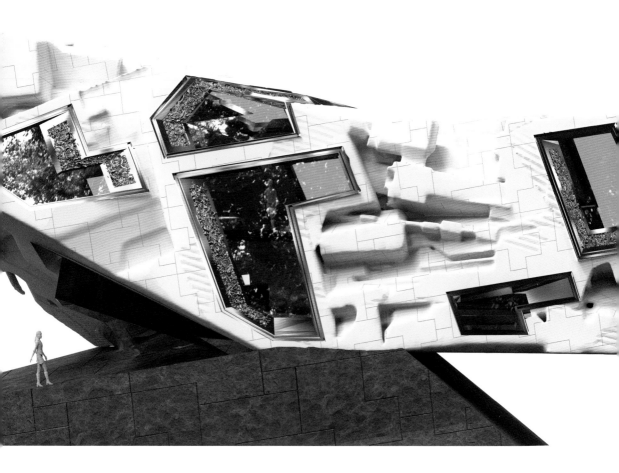

idea because it's about political equality, and each religion is represented by a side." That would be a concept defining the nature of a building, rather than its aesthetic qualities. The concept only works if you have knowledge about the tribes and knowledge about an octagon. We try to create buildings to be accessible and at least understandable at an intuitive level without ever having to understand a "concept" per se. The alternative to thinking about architecture through concepts, is thinking about architecture through aesthetics. This branch of philosophy largely comes from Immanuel Kant who introduced us to the idea of aesthetic judgment in the late 18th century. Kant says that you recognize a vase to be beautiful before you recognize it to be Middle Eastern, or as gold, or as porcelain. You make an aesthetic judgment

before you recognize what that thing is, before any concepts kick in. Therefore, humans have access to aesthetic qualities prior to conceptual ones, making them less contingent on knowledge and therefore more equal in their ability to be accessed. Once I recognize it as a "vase" I know that it has to hold water and has a particular function. We have equal access to aesthetic enjoyment, but we don't share equal access to conceptual enjoyment. If I say, "the Yale Center for British Art is all about democracy because there are no rooms and hierarchy. For the most part, and you can move all of the panels and it's reconfigurable," that it's somehow, "an idea about the constantly changing idea of art and that nothing is stable," that's another concept.

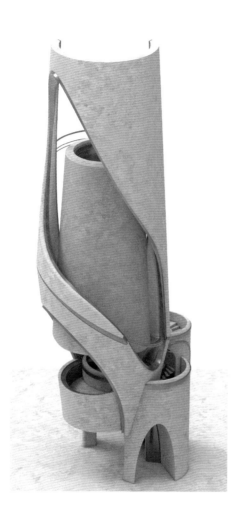 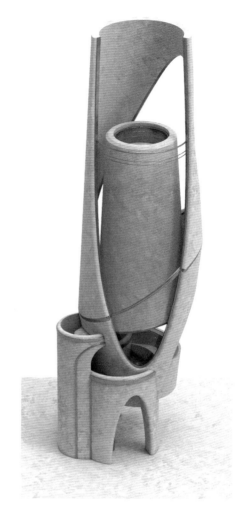

Maybe it's a good concept and maybe I like the concept, but it's also a concept that's not accessible to everyone. The interesting thing about aesthetics, is that they are universally accessible. I'm never interested in having one reading of my work.

Claude Rains: Could you talk about this idea as it relates to an actual project?

Mark Foster Gage: The one project which is probably the boldest in this interest in discrete objects and aesthetic readings is our Helsinki Guggenheim. The building is constituted from a bunch of 3D digital objects combined in a rather haphazard way. This, to start off with, is very anti-parametric. All the little parts have no relationships to one another. They are random objects,

randomly arranged. Secondly, there are so many objects and so many relationships that it would be impossible to imbue the building with any singular "correct" meaning because everybody can take meaning out of that project in a unique way. There's so much stuff going on in that project that if I asked my mom, "What do you think that project means?" She's going to say something completely unpredictable, and entirely different from the next person I ask. I'm really excited about that difference. I don't want a project to have one meaning so I'm interested in producing a complex aesthetic that has certain resonance with a culture, but ultimately it's the viewer that does the reading and decides what it's about. This is the opposite of the architect operating in an authoritarian way, imposing meaning. The alternative is what I call an "invitation to curiosity." When you produce this thing in the world that has more unusual or complex qualities than viewers are used to seeing, that produces an invitation for you to ask more questions about it, to read into it, to take away what you want to take away from it.

Claude Rains: How does this relationship between curiosity, labor, and unpredictability allow for certain ideas to enter the design process?

Mark Foster Gage: Every project is different, because on every project we're working with a different design language. Again, you'd be much better off as an architect designing your language and doing every project over and over in it. As tidy as it sounds, I just particularly love the process of design. I want to spend as much time in that process as possible. With every project we're designing a different workflow and sometimes this involves discovering a new software, maybe a mathematical software, or medical software, or AI. We try to figure out how alternative methods might help architects access different formal languages than they wouldn't normally have access to. One critique behind this is that currently most architects, at least in the United States, use BIM and maybe Rhino if they're lucky. That gives the architect a very limited palette of shapes and materials to work with. If you go one step further, corporations produce materials like wall panels or curtain walls that are increasingly adaptable for the architect to basically drag and drop them into BIM software. Not only are your tools limited to the software you're using, but the way you drag and drop corporate products to decorate those boxes is also very limited. Our entire urban structure is being defined, not by the imagination of architects, but by the limitations of tool developers and the corporate production of products. Generally, our work tries to not rely on those built-in features in software. This means we don't build a lot and that's fine. We build what we can, but we're more interested in pushing in new directions, because architecture isn't only about working with clients to solve their problems. Architecture is responsible for producing the backdrop of reality in which humans exist. Yes, we're meeting with clients, yes we're solving their individual problems, but we also have a larger responsibility to build that physical framework of reality. Over half the total global human population now lives in cities. By definition, these cities are defined by architecture. The world needs far more tools to address this design problem and, in a sense, we are toolmakers as much as architectural-project-producers.

Claude Rains: What does your current software toolkit include?

Mark Foster Gage: We use Rhino, Maya, Keyshot, Z-Brush, Mandelbulb 3D for fractals, different AI programs, DALL-E, and Midjourney or simple style-transfer apps like Ostagram. We use programs like Meshmixer that are designed to manage super high-poly models. All our models have millions upon millions of polygons and not many software programs can manage those files. We use programs like ZBrush quite a bit because ZBrush is capable of managing millions and millions of polygons. The software investment can get rather steep. For a while we were using AliasStudio, an automotive design program that was $50,000 per seat. We didn't pay that because I called them and told them I was an architect and I was interested in seeing how their software could help design architecture. It helps when

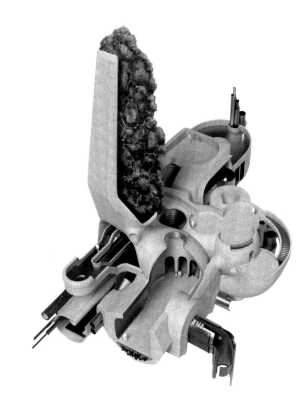

you describe the industry as a three-trillion dollar a year market. So I asked if they would be interested in seeing their software's potential within architecture. You'd be surprised what you can get from corporations by telling them you noticed that they have a really great product that you see potential for in architecture. It's a good way to form more experimental partnerships with industry and we do that quite a bit. I've had enormous luck with that strategy. This includes the things that

Claude Rains: Outside of efficiency-based processes, artificial intelligence in architecture is largely uncharted aesthetic territory. How does an AI workflow reinforce your interest in aesthetics during the architectural design process?

Mark Foster Gage: As you mentioned, AI in architecture is in its infancy. What I think is interesting about AI is its use as a design tool. I know how it's going to be used in architecture to make things even cheaper; eventually an AI is going to look at your building design and figure out a way to use 10% less plumbing, 10% less steel, move the bathrooms closer to the people, etc. For that reason, I anticipate AI is going to just continue to ruin architecture, because it's going to be used as an optimization tool that simply figures out how to make things faster and less expensive. Less creativity, more consistency, with the cheapest products and processes. It's exactly how non-AI software was used for architecture in the 1990s. There was hope that it would revolutionize our cities by enabling new forms of creativity, and it largely didn't. It did, however, revolutionize how we manage economics and financial performance. We wanted magic and we got BIM. My guess is that AI is going to be used as an optimization tool, but I'm really interested in its ability to design things that humans can't. Humans have a really amazing ability to recognize patterns, but we have zero ability to fuse patterns, and that's

we built for H&M and Lady Gaga. A lot of that stuff has been done through interesting and new materials or technical products, that were donated or discounted. I've never had a budget that was sufficient to build what I wanted to build, so I always had to find ways to get people to donate materials or expertise. Budgets are very rarely capable of building decent things, and they're almost never capable of building the kind of complex things that I'm interested in doing. Again, that means that we don't build a lot. When we do build, we have to find ways to work around budgets to get what we want.

one thing that AI is really good at. We are using AI to begin to fuse together two- and three-dimensional forms and patterns in ways that the human mind isn't capable of doing. For now, that's done in two dimensions through images or a really weak 3D, almost like an embossed form. AI isn't developed enough to do it in three full architectural dimensions. I'm not necessarily saying that we should use AI for buildings because it's cool. AI is just another tool that we can use to help shift ourselves out of our current creative blinders and it can put us into new types of imaginative territory. We shouldn't use a tool just because it's new, we should use new tools because they open up unexplored creative avenues for architects.

Claude Rains: You use language like "random" and "haphazard," but you've also described your design process as "labor intensive." Can you speak on this brute-force methodology further? How do you staff an office when different workflows are expanding and contracting across multiple projects?

Mark Foster Gage: Regarding the brute-force aspect of your question, my office is usually around eight people, and the largest it's ever been was seventeen people. On top of that, as expertise gets spread around the world, I'm finding that we're doing more project-by-project collaborations with people very far away. Currently we have collaborators in India, Singapore,

Beijing, and Vienna. I know people in these various places, a lot of former students, a lot of people I've met at symposia. If I am doing certain projects that require specific skills I reach out and we collaborate over distances. If I need to do something using a specific software program I won't necessarily learn it myself. Instead, I'll collaborate with someone who's already an expert in it.

Yuyi Shen: I'm interested in your decision making mechanisms in the office. How do you decide which iteration you go with, out of the hundreds you generate? What

else determines the eligibility of different objects?

Mark Foster Gage: It's very easy to recognize when forms, colors, patterns, and materials are sympathetic with the cultural or branded aspects of our projects. It's intuitive mostly, and collaborative. We discuss various options, and how we think they'll operate in the world. We don't discuss the process, or our concept, or refer to our diagrams. We speculate on how the building will interact with viewers and users in cultural registers. That said, sometimes when we're working in regions that are very foreign to us, we try to hire people from those

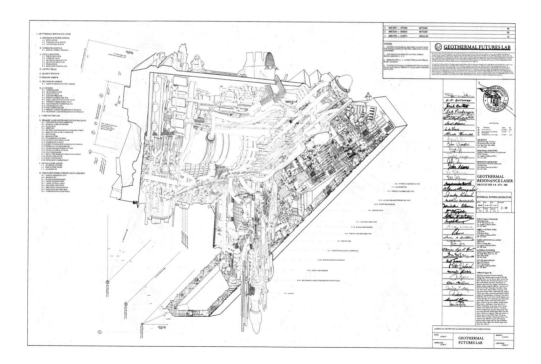

regions who have a nuanced eye to judge something like the difference between Persian and Saudi patterning. That's actually an example from a recent project. You really don't want to get those mixed up, for political reasons. It's incredibly nuanced. Someone in our office, Bashayer, was super helpful. There were times I would think something looked super interesting and beautiful and she would say it was too Persian, when it was supposed to be Saudi in character. Not literally, but just vaguely. I would ask what it meant and she told me she couldn't really explain it. It was super interesting. I could unpack a classical building in New York, I can take it back to Rome and Greece, tell you the difference between metopes and triglyphs, different degrees of entasis, I'm an expert on all of it. That said, I have had zero non-western education in terms of history. It just wasn't available when I was in school. Thus, I have zero sensibility with regards to those architectural languages. It's just another reason we should include these non-western traditions in history courses. It gives us a much larger palette of materials to be creative with. I can't tell you how frustrating it was

Discussion with
Mark Foster Gage and **Claude Rains**

for me to not be able to see what she was talking about. We treat expertise seriously. In the same way, you would hire a pastry chef if you want to make desserts because they are better with pastries and sugar than a regular chef. Even though someone may be the most famous chef in the world, they might not do so well with sugar. You have to find the expertise that you need and collaborate, collaborate, collaborate. We did the Peru National Museum competition, and I just happened to go to school with a friend who is Peruvian and her dad was an architect. I would casually send her images for her opinions. The worst thing I could do is design and present something that I think is Saudi, when it isn't. If you are an amateur cutting and pasting minarets and domes, you are essentially making a kind of pseudo theme park of a Saudi project or a Bedouin project. That's cultural appropriation in the worst way. We're more interested in making contemporary projects with a vague and subtle nod to cultural and regional histories.

Samar Halloum: Do you think it is better that architecture students know a bit about everything, passing up a chance to go into depth? Or would you suggest striving for expertise in one area?

Mark Foster Gage: The great Oxford philosopher and literary critic Isaiah Berlin once wrote a book about Leo Tolstoy called *The Hedgehog and the Fox*, which I believe was originally from a fable. The fox was a person who knew a little about everything and nothing in depth. The hedgehog knew one thing in depth, but not much about anything else. One wasn't necessarily better than the other, for instance, the names of historic hedgehogs: Plato, Proust, Nietzsche, Dostoyevsly, Hegel, Plato, and Dante. He also names historic foxes: James Joyce, Balzac, Pushkin, Goethe, Moliere, and Aristotle. These are only partial lists of what he recites, but my point is that the discipline of literature benefitted immensely from both, as the wildly

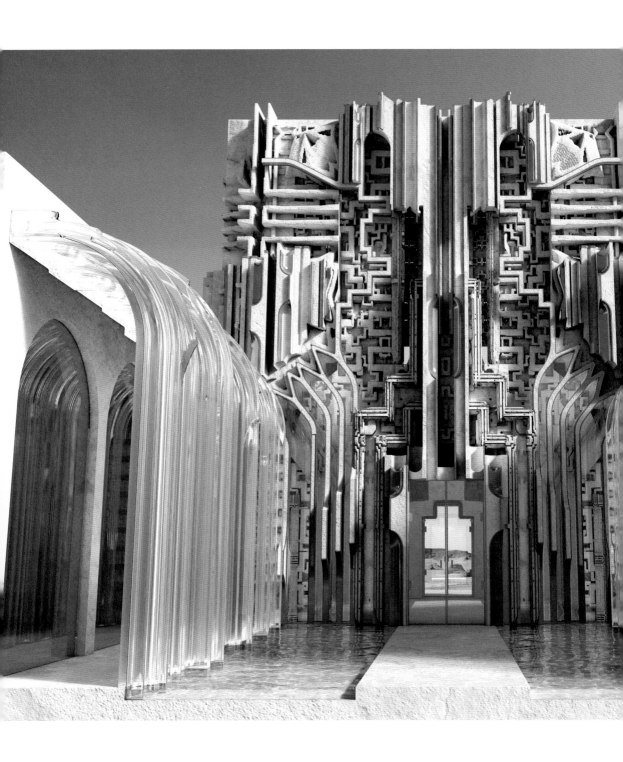

Discussion with
Mark Foster Gage and **Claude Rains**

varied work of these figures can attest to. Of course, when discussing a historic idea of cannon like this we need to be cognizant of the voices left out of the equation by virtue of sex and race, but the idea spotlights a very interesting question for architecture. I wonder if someone wrote a book called "The Hedgehog and the Fox: Architectural Edition," which people would fall into which camp. Having said all of this, I'm a fox. While I have expertise in certain things, like aesthetics or classical form, it's not at the expense of knowing other things. I love physics, especially quantum discoveries, astronomy, and etymologies, but only as an amateur. Architecture benefits from knowledge about many things, but that can happen in the individual architect, or through collaboration between experts. If I was designing my own architecture school I would want to incorporate at least one survey course that went very shallow into a whole bunch of traditions, and then I would let people choose to go deep in certain areas. I wish I had such a thing in school. It wasn't until recently that I discovered some amazing historic architecture that I had never even heard about in these incredible necropolis structures in Uzbekistan, some of which are a millennium old. Why had I never been introduced to them in a theory class? I actually went to Uzbekistan a few years ago to see them, in Samarkand. I've taken classes on vaulting and stone architecture and I know everything about a very small and specific amount of Western classicism as it goes from Greece to Rome into Europe to the United States. How did I not come across this incredible Uzbek corbelling and vaulting? I would have taken a class only on that if it had been available because it's so much more intricate than western domes and apses. I would have taken a really deep dive into that really specific area had it been available, but it wasn't. There is a value in giving people, especially in an architectural education, a shallow survey of a lot more of what exists in the world. It's actually really frustrating to me when I see that most of the history classes offered in architecture schools are really only about the history of western architectural modernism. Start out in fox classes and later take hedgehog classes as you learn what interests you.

Stav Dror: Your work relies significantly on renderings, which obviously cost money. How is it sustainable to develop such a high volume of photo realistic images?

Mark Foster Gage: In my twenty-year career we've probably only commissioned

twenty renderings. Almost all of what we do is in-house. My first architecture job was as a watercolor renderer, so I have a good grasp on at least the manual, paintbrush version of that field. A lot of those skills are transferrable to a digital world; how light behaves, how materials behave, etc. In order to learn how to shift from a paper world to a digital world, over the years I've also personally taken online courses from Hollywood professionals on the subject of Matte painting. This is for work but crosses over as a little bit of a hobby for me. The long and short of it, is that we do them in-house because I enjoy doing them. It saves a ton of money, but it does take quite a bit of time to do the photo-realism that we do. It would be much easier if I did boxy axonometric on pastel pink backgrounds as seems to be the rage these days. Yet I persist…

Stav Dror: To achieve this level of intricacy in your projects, clearly your clients have to be incredibly rich.

Mark Foster Gage: Either they have to be rich or you have to be clever about how you organize the process. The level of exposure

you will get from a project is a form of currency in itself. You do not always need to have a rich client to make the things that you want, even if they look expensive. We do it mostly by collaborating with companies to push their products and materials farther. It becomes a form of research and development to them, and we get things either free or at a discounted rate.

Stav Dror: As an architect, do you see your work as a political tool? Do you perceive your practice as political?

Mark Foster Gage: The way my practice is political is largely conveyed in a book I wrote, titled *Designing Social Equality: Architecture, Aesthetics and the Perception of Democracy*. Baudrillard says that all architecture is about the exertion of power, as architecture is the most expensive thing on earth and only the very richest can afford it. I don't know if that's entirely true. We also try to find local expertise and labor. An example of this is in the previously mentioned project in Saudi Arabia we were proposing stone carving techniques that were historically used in the area. This is political, in that you can choose who profits from your work. You can utilize those whose community the building is in, or you can have things shipped from thousands of miles away where the profit goes to China or corporations with headquarters halfway around the world. Regarding power, I'm not sure how you get away from that double-edged sword in

Discussion with
Mark Foster Gage and **Claude Rains**

architecture. On one hand, we are one of the most public disciplines. Everyone can look at architecture for free and we're one of the best disciplines for creating jobs. At the same time, we're also one of the best disciplines for exerting power and privilege. I think that is a disciplinary problem, and one that's made more explicit recently given the increasing income gaps emerging globally. Architects will always need to juggle these kinds of impacts. I am writing a book about ethics and architecture currently and I would say, without a doubt, architects should be taking courses in ethics.

When you use the system of the status-quo, you're unwittingly complicit in some unethical behavior by virtue of the process. We have to know more about what we're doing, know more about the choices available, and be willing to make the right ones.

Stav Dror: And do you have this power dynamic in mind when you work?

Mark Foster Gage: I always have it in mind. I wrote a book about it, but I would not say I have any definitive universal answers yet. If you consider the Burj Khalifa

Discussion with
Mark Foster Gage and **Claude Rains**

in Dubai, that is a serious exerting of authority which is mostly for the benefit of government, offices, and corporations and that has less of a cultural value. The Burj Khalifa is a pure expression of power, and I don't know if I'm ethical enough to turn down a project like that. My ego and bank account would want me to do it, but my ethical and moral compass might not. Perhaps the best way to go about it is to accept it knowing that you can introduce as many ethical practices into the process as possible. Perhaps another architect who gets the project might not.

Vicky Achnani: You have mentioned that your practice doesn't build often, but building is also a form of feedback that informs practice in a unique way. What is your fundamental reason for not building?

Mark Foster Gage: I love designing, thinking, writing, and teaching. I am good at those things. What I am not good at is filling my days with back-to-back meetings and hustling at cocktail parties. In the beginning of my practice I hated cold calling people about potential projects. These are the things you need to do in order to have a large practice and build a lot. You need to be the kind of person who likes being out in the world, flying all over the place, having tons of meetings, drinking Chardonnay while trying to meet people for new projects, etc. I am not this person. People who want our design sensibility contact us. We don't ambulance chase. I

don't judge people who do that, but it's not what I want my life to be. I'd rather have a life of the mind than a life of the meeting. We have enough projects and we also turn down a lot of projects, but we are also not building skyscrapers. I don't have the kind of ego that plans to build a skyscraper in order to feel like I've "arrived." I do not have that need. I also simply don't think it's going to happen. You have to carve out a life that you enjoy and not let other people's ideas of success define you. My life will have been successful and meaningful even without building a ton or getting a Pritzker.

Ingrid Liu: What types of projects do you typically turn down?

Mark Foster Gage: We get a lot of people who want to do residential projects. They will see something we have done before, like this $20 million USD penthouse in Soho we designed, and they want us to do their apartment. The problem is they often have a bunch of magazine clippings and request a house or apartment that looks like something specific. Obviously, we can do a really great house like that. I could knock out a killer Tuscan villa by virtue of my background in classical architecture, but I usually give those kinds of projects to architect friends who do more focused work on that kind of thing. If we get a client that's not interested in innovating and thinking about how to do something within contemporary cultural value, then I

don't want to do the project. I'm not interested in projects that serve an individual client only; I don't want to do projects that don't have a larger cultural or architectural ambition to be important in some way. We are doing this small library in Shropshire England for a client of ours, and we have been working on it for several years. It's been through all the approvals, all the way up through multiple levels of the UK parliament, because it's such a historic site. It includes a house built in 1531, and it's the site of a former 12th-century templar chapel. I remember asking my client why he chose me, and he said he was going to buy a new pre-Raphaelite painting but then he realized if he bought a painting, he would just be taking care of culture. What he wanted to do was create something that produced and added to culture. So he started studying architects and finding architects he thought would add something new to culture. What an enlightened client, to say he doesn't want to care for culture but that he wants to add to culture. He whittled it down to five architects that he thought could add something to architecture and artistic culture, and I was part of that group. When I asked him why he chose me he told me it was mostly because I was still alive, as many of the architects whose work he liked were dead already. I ended up getting the project because I wasn't dead. Wanting to "add something to culture" was such a beautiful way of phrasing his intentions. That is the ideal client, and that's a box we want checked with every project we do. We want to add something to culture.

Discussion with
Mark Foster Gage and **Claude Rains**

Elise Limon: If you weren't an architect, what would you be? Is that something that you fantasize about?

Mark Foster Gage: I think about this all the time. I'd probably be involved in constitutional law. I love physics and astronomy but am simply not smart enough to make an impact in those disciplines. To be honest, I just plain suck at math. I am, however, excellent with precedent. I have an encyclopedic memory for architectural precedent, which is probably why my work often has a historic flavor. Constitutional law is another discipline that is precedent-heavy. I would love constructing arguments out of previous rulings. I think I'd like to be the person who argues in front of the Supreme Court. Not a justice, but the lawyer arguing for one side of what they are considering. Constitutional issues and how they relate to history is something I find particularly exciting, in a totally nerdy way. Sometimes I regret not going that route, when it seems like that's so much more important in the world, but ultimately I made the right decision. Architecture has been great to me. I do have to say that there's certainly frustration with the financial aspect. Architects often watch their non-architect friends get consistently richer than them over time. I mean architects can make good money, you can have a great life and a good living, but you very rarely make that kind of money hedge-fund managers make.

Yuyi Shen: Why is symmetry so frequently in your work?

Mark Foster Gage: I had a professor once at Notre Dame, a classical architect, who said, "always design symmetrical buildings, because you only have to design half a building." I'm also just naturally drawn to it. Perhaps this is because I spent so much time designing and studying classical architecture, but I also find it something that's just unusual today. Why aren't there more symmetrical buildings? I don't really buy that idea that symmetrical buildings are somehow more authoritarian because there's only one privileged point of access, like how the Congress is symmetrical and the Supreme Court is symmetrical. I don't really buy the political reasons for not doing symmetry that modernism provided us with. As Greg Lynn says, "it's the cheapest form of beauty." I guarantee if you have an ugly project on your screen, throw it in Photoshop and make it symmetrical and it's going to look a lot better. It just became a thing and now it's almost like a little signature and everyone kind of expects it. For whatever reason, I am now the most symmetrical guy in architecture.

Claudia Ansorena: How do you reconcile trying to create a specific formal language with a cultural progression defined by more urgent and present problems, such as housing, to name one example?

Mark Foster Gage: Well, I think that's a common misconception, that architects have the ability to just choose to do housing and do a lot of housing. The power that creates solutions to those problems does not come from architecture, it comes from policy. I think the solution for architects is to get more involved in policy. You can't really say you want to build 200 units of low-income housing and then go find a client to pay for it. I suppose you could, but architecture is the one art that, by definition, is shared by communities. I think it's a little bit too easy to say that the pressing problems of today always trump the need for cultural value in the communities of today. A good example of that is during the refugee crisis, architecture studios in schools around the US were all developing refugee housing. I know this because I was on half of the reviews. If you look at studies on refugee housing, they have some of the highest depression rates in the world. This is because they aren't really homes, and it's also because they're relentlessly repetitive and have no cultural qualities whatsoever. Should we be designing refugee housing that are all identical on a grid over 20 acres? Or should we think about solutions to problems that integrate those people into communities where culture is also present in the urban fabric in which they exist. It seems like the problem is always divided, where aesthetics is seen as frivolous and construction of housing is what we need to be doing more of. The industry doesn't think about things like cultural value and community.

Claude Rains: You mentioned turning down projects, is that difficult for you?

Mark Foster Gage: It's hard to step away and say you're not the right person for a job. If I was commissioned to do a Museum of Black History in New York City, I would, of course, decline. I'm obviously not the right person for that job, even though I would sure love to have something like that as a project. I'm just not nearly as versed in what such a project would entail and the meaning it would hold, especially when so many other architects would. It's hard for the ego to step aside and make room for others to do things that you aren't the best at. It is difficult, as you suggest, but it's both the right thing for me to do architecturally, and in certain cases, it might be the correct thing for me to do ethically. I remember, I was one of five finalists to be the dean at Pratt a number of years ago and I met with the Provost of Diversity and Inclusion in one of our meetings. She asked what the most impactful decision would be in order to open up the school's leadership positions to more diverse candidates. My answer was, "don't hire me."

Afterword

Cynthia Davidson

Afterword, n. Originally: a later word; a word (or passage) printed or spoken after another. Now usually: a passage added at the end of a book or other work, containing concluding remarks or similar additional matter. Cf. FOREWORD *n.*, POSTSCRIPT *n.*[1] 1.

Afterview, n. The action or an act of reconsidering or reflecting on a past event, activity, etc.; a retrospective or subsequent view on or of something. Cf. FORE-VIEW *n.*

– Oxford English Dictionary

To conclude a book of conversations with a written rather than oral response feels a bit like being late to a party. If you weren't at the party, what can you really say about it? Sure, I've been party *to* aspects of some of these conversations, but in a different context, and at different times. So rather than an afterword, I'd like to propose an afterview, something more retrospective or subsequent than concluding, particularly since this volume promises a sense of "what's next."

Twenty years ago, under the auspices of the Anyone Corporation, an architecture think tank, I launched a new architecture periodical called *Log: Observations on Architecture and the Contemporary City.* Similar to a ship's log, this *Log* set out to record critical movements in architecture and urban planning in the 21st century. The crisis in architecture that David Ruy says now "feels real" felt real back then too. The first issue to roll off the presses, in September 2003, was partially in response to the design proposals for the site of the World Trade Center towers, which had been destroyed by a terrorist attack on September 11, 2001. One of the first proposals for rebuilding, by Peterson Littenberg Architects, included setback towers and gardens that recalled the aesthetic of prewar New York and the urban ideals of the École des Beaux-Arts. In contrast, the twisting strands that composed a monumental tower proposed by United Architects (a team that included Greg Lynn) seemed to take a technological leap into an unpredictable future. The glassy towers on the WTC site today represent a certain status quo of big business that has no patience for the debates over the hegemony of modernism, the fragmentation of deconstruction, or the rapid advance of the digital [virtual?] in architecture. Ironically, the Peterson Littenberg and United Architects schemes stimulated more debate about the future of architecture and the city than the Daniel Libeskind master plan and the ensuing towers designed by established global architecture firms. What does that say about the crisis of architecture?

Hundreds of conversations about architecture, in both essay and interview form, have appeared in *Log*'s pages. And over time, their focus has changed: from theory to research; from the postcritical to the postdigital; from sustainability to the climate crisis; from the problem of representation to physics engines; from aesthetics of form to the aesthetics of social justice; and more. Somehow, architecture itself—design, aesthetics, construction, criticism—got sidetracked, lost in the storm of socioeconomic and environmental problems it is now both blamed for and challenged to resolve.

I am a baby boomer. My millennial sons have both told me that my generation created today's problems, but that their generation will fix them (neither is an architect). One of the problems they may not recognize, however, is that how we communicate, how we receive and process information, how we design and even build—things generally seen as technological advances—was also shaped by baby boomers (Steve Jobs, Bill Gates, for example). What will millennials do about that?

To conclude his book *Theory and Design in the First Machine Age*, published in 1960, critic Reyner Banham wrote: "The architect who proposes to run with technology knows now that he will be in fast company, and that, in order to keep up, he may have to emulate the Futurists and discard his whole cultural load, including the professional garments by which he is recognised as an architect. If, on the other hand, he decides not to do this, he may find that a technological culture has decided to go on without him."

Today, the architect reinventing a practice to address 21st-century concerns once again seems challenged to "discard [their] cultural load," but not to keep up with technology. Digital technology is us, embedded in the body, the brain, the city, the farm, and cradled in the palms of our hands.

In architecture, as Kristy Balliet notes in this book, the digital is now a territory to be explored rather than simply a methodology for production. David Ruy and Karel Klein's early experiments in training Artificial Intelligence (AI) to produce images on command is one exploration of such a digital territory. On the other hand, architect Neil Leach's recent exchange with the AI program ChatGPT, published in *Dezeen* in February 2023, "forecast" a whole other territory. According to Leach, ChatGPT wrote:

"In the near future, architects may become a thing of the past. *Artificial intelligence (AI) is quickly advancing to a point where it can generate the design of a building completely autonomously. With the potential to create designs faster and with more accuracy than ever before, AI has the potential to revolutionize the architecture industry, leaving traditional architects out of the equation. This could spell the end of the profession as we know it, raising questions of what the future holds for architects in a world of AI-generated buildings."*

Perhaps having learned from Banham's warning, ChatGPT continued: "Architects who choose to ignore AI will be left behind and ultimately forgotten as the industry evolves and advances. Therefore, it is imperative that architects pay attention to AI and its potential to revolutionize architecture, or they risk sleepwalking into oblivion."

History shows that technology has always shaped the general culture regardless of geography, and thus the relationship of architecture to that culture. The technologies that inform the conversations here will also become part of history—in a matter of moments. Leach, summing up his ChatGPT exchange, writes, "Surely, what we architects should be designing right now is not another building, but rather the very future of our profession."

Contemplating the future—the "what's next"—always involves the question of history. Not only the history of human knowledge that constitutes the foundational models of AI, but also, for architects, the history of architecture itself. In his "Theses on the Philosophy of History," written in 1940, Walter Benjamin describes Paul Klee's *Angelus Novus* as being blown backward into the future by a storm called Progress, its eyes on the detritus of history at its feet. Will AI always be sifting human history to produce a future that, like Benjamin's angel, neither we, nor it, can actually see? Today, even in the current expansionist mode of revisionism that is exposing centuries of exclusion and repression, architectural history still has touchstones—Vitruvius's *Ten Books* being one. As Mark Foster Gage says, "part of architectural discourse is having dialogues with architects that may have been dead for centuries." Ferda Kolatan, thinking about hybridity, rather than ideology, in architecture, discusses how history crept into and enriched his work with the digital. Investigating the uses of architectural materials, Ellie Abrons realized materials have narratives—i.e., histories; Michael Young wants architecture to "redistribute our assumptions about the way in which reality appears," an age-old architectural problem that began with the oblique drawing.

The storm called Progress leads to instability and banality, demystification and mythmaking, irony and sincerity—all conditions and concepts addressed in the conversations here. Arguably, if Jacques Derrida's theory of deconstruction made a meaningful contribution to architecture, it was not the aesthetic of fragmentation but the idea of instability, or undecidability, that has lasting value. The undecidable does not preclude decisions; rather, as a concept it broadens the possibilities for interpretation and action.

Deconstruction may already be history, but its effects underlie how architecture addresses the conditions and concepts that could change the history of the future—of architecture and of culture in general. The unpredictability of conversations and the questions they raise offer one important path forward.

Image credits:
We are grateful to those designers and architects who have allowed us to reproduce images from their archives, as follows:

Chapter 1:
All images property of David Ruy and Karel Klein

Chapter 2:
Images property of Mitch McEwen (41,43, 54-55)
and Amina Blacksher (38-39,46,48)

Chapter 3:
Images property of Ferda Kolatan / SU11 with the exception of Page 58: Oddkin Architecture Istanbul (2019) Design Studio by Ferda Kolatan, TA: Michael Zimmerman, Students: Caleb Ehly & Joonsung Lee, Univ. of Pennsylvania Weitzman School of Design, Page 61: Misfits Cairo (2017). Design Studio by Ferda Kolatan, TA: Michael Zimmerman, Students: Angela Huang & Alex Tahinos, Univ. of Pennsylvania Weitzman School of Design and Page 72: Oddkin Architecture Istanbul (2018). Design Studio by Ferda Kolatan, TA: Michael Zimmerman, Students: Yuanyi Zhou & Wenjia Go, Univ. of Pennsylvania Weitzman School of Design

Chapter 4:
All images property of Tom Wiscombe Architecture

Chapter 5:
All images property of T+E+A+M

Chapter 6:
All images property of Young & Ayata

Chapter 7:
All images property of Jimenez Lai (153-156, 159, 161, 167-172, 179), and Kristy Balliet (157, 158, 163-166, 173-178)

Chapter 8:
Images property of Elena Manferdini (183, 185, 188-193)
and Florencia Pita (181, 182, 184, 187, 195-199)

Chapter 9:
All images property of Mark Foster Gage

ORO Editions

Publishers of Architecture, Art, and Design
Gordon Goff: Publisher

www.oroeditions.com
info@oroeditions.com

Published by ORO Editions

Author: Mark Foster Gage
Managing Editor and Book Design: Christopher Pin and MFGA
Project Manager: Jake Anderson

10 9 8 7 6 5 4 3 2 1 First Edition

ISBN: 978-1-957183-18-3

Color Separations and Printing: ORO Group Inc.
Printed in China.

ORO Editions makes a continuous effort to minimize the overall carbon foot-
print of its publications. As part of this goal, ORO, in association with Global
ReLeaf, arranges to plant trees to replace those used in the manufacturing of the
paper produced for its books. Global ReLeaf is an international campaign run
by American Forests, one of the world's oldest nonprofit conservation organizations. Global ReLeaf is American Forests' education and action program that
helps individuals, organizations, agencies, and corporations improve the local
and global environment by planting and caring for trees.